T0330795

Global Entrepreneurship Analytics

This innovative book proposes new methodologies for the measurement of entrepreneurship by applying techniques of demography, engineering, mathematics and statistics.

Using the data from the Global Entrepreneurship Monitor (GEM), statistical demographic techniques are used for the evaluation of data quality (EDQ), and a new methodology for the estimation of Specific Entrepreneurship Rates (SER) and the Global Entrepreneurship Rate (GER) is proposed. At the same time the authors present artificial intelligence techniques such as Fuzzy Time Series (FTS) to forecast data series of the entrepreneurial population. Finally, they present a case study of the implementation of Big Data in Entrepreneurship using GEM data that shows the latest technological trends for the management of data, in support of making more accurate decisions. Being a methodological book, the techniques presented can be applied to any dataset in different areas. Readers will learn new methodologies of analysis and measurement of entrepreneurship using data from the Global Entrepreneurship Monitor. They will be able to access the experience of the authors through each of the applied cases in which the reader is taken by the hand, both through the scientific method and through the methodology of construction of more accurate metrics in entrepreneurship, with less error.

This book will be of value to students at an advanced level, academics and researchers in the fields of Entrepreneurship, Business Analytics and Research Methodology.

Milenka Linneth Argote Cusi is Founder of Business Intelligence and Demography SAS (www.bidem.com.co).

León Darío Parra Bernal is Associate Professor at EAN University, Bogotá, Colombia (www.universidadean.edu.co).

Routledge Focus on Business and Management

The fields of business and management have grown exponentially as areas of research and education. This growth presents challenges for readers trying to keep up with the latest important insights. Routledge Focus on Business and Management presents small books on big topics and how they intersect with the world of business research.

Individually, each title in the series provides coverage of a key academic topic, while collectively the series forms a comprehensive collection across the business disciplines.

Distributed Leadership and Digital Innovation
The Argument for Couple Leadership
Caterina Maniscalco

Public Relations Crisis Communication
A New Model
Lisa Anderson-Meli and Swapna Koshy

Implicative Marketing
For a Sustainable Economy
Florence Touzé

Global Entrepreneurship Analytics
Using GEM Data
Milenka Linneth Argote Cusi and León Darío Parra Bernal

For more information about this series, please visit: www.routledge.com/Routledge-Focus-on-Business-and-Management/book-series/FBM

Global Entrepreneurship Analytics

Using GEM Data

Milenka Linneth Argote Cusi and León Darío Parra Bernal

Routledge
Taylor & Francis Group

NEW YORK AND LONDON

First published 2021
by Routledge
52 Vanderbilt Avenue, New York, NY 10017

and by Routledge
2 Park Square, Milton Park, Abingdon, Oxon OX14 4RN

*Routledge is an imprint of the Taylor & Francis Group, an
informa business*

© 2021 Taylor & Francis

The right of Milenka Linneth Argote Cusi and León Darío
Parra Bernal to be identified as authors of this work has been
asserted by them in accordance with sections 77 and 78 of the
Copyright, Designs and Patents Act 1988.

All rights reserved. No part of this book may be reprinted or
reproduced or utilised in any form or by any electronic,
mechanical, or other means, now known or hereafter invented,
including photocopying and recording, or in any information
storage or retrieval system, without permission in writing from
the publishers.

Trademark notice: Product or corporate names may be
trademarks or registered trademarks, and are used only for
identification and explanation without intent to infringe.

Library of Congress Cataloging-in-Publication Data
Names: Argote Cusi, Milenka Linneth, author. | Parra Bernal,
León Darío, author.
Title: Global entrepreneurship analytics : using GEM data /
Milenka Linneth Argote Cusi, León Darío Parra Bernal.
Description: New York, NY : Routledge, 2021. |
Series: Routledge focus on business and management | Includes
bibliographical references and index.
Identifiers: LCCN 2020016116 | ISBN 9780367321178
(hardback) | ISBN 9780429316715 (ebook)
Subjects: LCSH: Entrepreneurship--Statistical methods.
Classification: LCC HB615 .A746 2021 | DDC 338/.040727--dc23
LC record available at https://lccn.loc.gov/2020016116

ISBN: 978-0-367-32117-8 (hbk)
ISBN: 978-0-429-31671-5 (ebk)

Typeset in Times New Roman
by MPS Limited, Dehradun

Dedicated to all those innovative researchers in the study of measurement methods for reducing uncertainty, especially for the Global Entrepreneurship Monitor whose worldwide initiative is a benchmark in the measurement of entrepreneurship.

Contents

Illustrations

Figures

Tables

Preface

The main motivation of this book is the application of new methodologies for the measurement of entrepreneurship. Consistent with the philosophy of entrepreneurship whose differential is innovation, it is necessary to innovate in new metrics on entrepreneurship in support of making more accurate decisions.

The measurement of entrepreneurship is not simple, since it is a complex concept that defines a state or action of the individual that is related to many factors, especially those of economics and survival. Thus, this book delves into the concepts of measurement and its practical application to discover a number or data that ultimately tries to measure as objectively as possible the phenomenon under study. There is no doubt that in order to make a "good" measurement, the rigor of the methods used should provide the scientific support required to have a level of confidence in the metrics generated.

Data is required for measurement. The issue of data is crucial, since it is the raw material used to create a measure. That is why, given the availability of official Global Entrepreneurship Monitor Data that collects information on entrepreneurship worldwide in a standardized way, this book uses this rich source of information in all chapters for the case of Colombia because it is available to the authors. It should be noted that the authors have tried to explain the methodologies presented in this book so that they can be applied using other databases or other cases, and that is the most important value of this intellectual production.

Being consistent with the thread of the book, it begins with a transcendental theme, before transforming the data into useful information for decision making, the Evaluation of Data Quality (EDQ) in Chapter 1. Thus, the book begins with a methodology for the evaluation of the quality of the data that uses statistical and demographic techniques and that was presented in its first version at the GEM data use seminar for scientific publications in 2018 held in Bogotá, Colombia.

Chapter 2 presents a new entrepreneurship metric, the Global Entrepreneurship Rate (GER), created similarly to the Global Fertility Rate, an internationally known indicator calculated in a standardized way worldwide for monitoring the number of children per woman. In this sense, the theoretical mathematical concepts of this rate are taken up and by analogy applied to the case of entrepreneurship to find a measure of the average annual number of ventures per adult between the ages of 18 and 64. Behind the GER summary indicator are the Specific Entrepreneurship Rates (SER) that are estimated and explained in this chapter. The metrics created are consistent and capture the heterogeneity of entrepreneurship behavior at different ages.

Chapter 2 is the input for Chapter 3. With a new metric on entrepreneurship that eliminates sample bias, Fuzzy Time Series (FTS) is applied to forecast GER data series using GEM data. It is an innovative methodology that comes from Artificial Intelligence (AI) which models with greater certainty phenomena that are not subject to assumptions such as linearity and balance. The importance of Chapter 3 is that it ventures into sophisticated techniques of forecasting methods that nowadays apply to organizations with a high level of maturity.

Chapter 4 takes another step in the use of new technologies for data management and the generation of new metrics, this time integrating different data sources. This chapter presents the methodology developed for the implementation of Big Data technologies for the exploitation of GEM data. The project, which was carried out between 2017–2018, has generated interesting lessons that can be taken into account to initiate and execute projects of this magnitude. The importance of this chapter is the transfer of knowledge in the implementation of projects in Big Data in general and its usefulness in the case of the GEM that would allow it to integrate information from different official sources of data, which constitute a valuable input for the construction of new, more complex metrics for decision making.

We hope that this book is an open source of future applications as well as a source of innovations that will allow us to leave our comfort zone, expand knowledge boundaries and integrate new methodologies from other areas which provide tools to perform measurement processes that are more accurate or otherwise contain less error.

Sincerely,

The Authors

1 Methodology for the Evaluation of Data Quality

The GEM Case

1.1 Introduction

A key process of data science is the stage prior to data analysis, namely the evaluation of data quality (EDQ). It is important to note that data science begins with the collection of data, without which we could not make science. There are several data collection methods: censuses, surveys, public records, and nowadays we can add data from social networks. Each of these methods entails its own scope and limits while using different techniques from statistics and demography.

Data quality control starts from its collection, which is why there are techniques that allow us to minimize error in the process of collection. Once the data is collected it is stored in databases called "microdata" that refer to the original data. The process of typing and organizing data in structures such as databases requires a particular knowledge of data design and management; in addition, knowledge of the technologies is also necessary to carry out this process efficiently (servers, database managers, software, hardware, etc.).

Once we have a set of organized and systematized data understandable to the "general public", the process that gives meaning to this chapter begins: the evaluation of data quality. In the frame of data science, the difference between Data Cleaning, Data Tidying, Data Mining and Data Analytics is that EDQ is applied after data is cleaned, organized and standardized and prior to DA. It is a stage in which specific techniques are applied that derive from the experience of the data scientist and the knowledge of the data source, and probably due to this it is a generally omitted phase in the different data science projects or applied studies, or a phase relegated to a technical aspect, when it is of vital importance for the validity and reliability of the data. If an EDQ is not performed, surely the information obtained from the data will be erroneous.

It is feasible to find in the literature researches on data quality in areas related to engineering and health, and there are methodological proposals, each from a different perspective. It is a process that depends on creativity and both the integral knowledge and techniques of the area to design instruments or processes (i.e., play with the data) with the objective of evidencing possible errors or inconsistencies in the information that can call into question the information obtained from the data. However, the experience in EDQ allows us to design a methodology that can be applied in any area.

1.2 The Data Contains Errors

It is important to accept that data contains errors; that is to say, it is perfectible. The analysis of uncertainty associated with data with the idea of collecting information for government, institutions or for scientific research is a challenge. In other words, from the moment the need for data arises, an abstraction level is born to design the instrument and select the techniques required to collect data according to the objective of the research or intervention.

Errors can be summarized into sample and non-sample errors during the process of collecting the information from the beginning until it is available in a database (Argote, 2003). In the conceptual phase of the idea or need to obtain data, errors are tied to the level of abstraction of the person who conceived it and they are expressed in concepts, definitions and measures that will be specified in a design. The design phase of the instrument or the data collection source is also subject to human error, since, if there is no good design of the instruments, the experiment will be unsuccessful. Another source of error is the selection of the population from whom the information referring to the sample design is collected, which may result in sample errors that limit the inferences that can be made from the data.

At the moment of the implementation of the fieldwork or of what the data entry itself is, there are several non-sampling errors tied to all the actors involved in the process such as surveyors, interviewers and supervisors, all of whom can make mistakes in their declarations or in the collection and verification processes. The data is collected in a repository depending on the available technology (e.g., paper, google forms, excel, etc.). There is a process of typing data that can lead to further human or interface errors. It is assumed that there is a database design behind the typing process, with certain quality requirements to ensure that data is organized so it can be optimally exploited later. However, this phase can still be subject to error if it is not done by a specialist in design and database management.

Finally, once the data is organized in structures that allow its manipulation by computational means, which is constituted in a product that includes or is the sum of the errors that could have accumulated during the process, consequently it is a product that should be evaluated.

1.3 What Is the Evaluation of Data Quality?

According to the literature, quality is a relative concept. The concept of quality arises in the production sector given the need to measure its goals not only by the level of production but also by the quality of each of the products offered to customers. In this sense, what is understood by quality in a given sector is defined by the interest group through different dimensions which are considered important for quality measurement. According to Heredia and Vilalta (2009), what can be quality for some may differ from quality for others; however, it should be oriented towards improvement.

Quality is a desired characteristic of things and products, since it is synonymous with well done, well dealt with, well built, etc. Heredia and Vilalta (2009), in their article on the importance of evaluating data quality for companies, define data quality on the basis of the implications of their poor quality. "Poor data quality affects business management in various ways. Obviously a primary affectation of the poor data quality is its effect on decision making."

In this regard data quality refers to the fact that data, as well as products and services, must have quality, as the implications of not possessing it affect accurate decision making. The evaluation of data quality is a process that involves different methodologies, techniques and technologies prior to its use in knowledge management (Heredia & Vilalta, 2009; Argote, 2003). The data quality measurements are conducted effectively through dimensions such as those mentioned by Hadhiatma (2018): namely completeness, consistency and precision. Other authors, depending on the area, use other dimensions within which the most important ones (which are taken into account in this chapter) are coherence, validity, truthfulness and reliability (Zúñiga & Sánchez, 2012; Azeroual, Saake & Abuosba, 2019; Hadhiatma, 2018).

1.4 Methodologies to Evaluate Data Quality (MEDC)

Given the different perspectives and data source, the methodologies are diverse; however, it is feasible to find points of convergence.

So, the literature has several EDQ cases mostly from the quantitative, engineering, information technology areas and others in the health and demography areas, demonstrating the extremes in which this field moves, from the very technical to the most social, making the intermediate areas such as entrepreneurship, that comes from the economy, lag behind in the application of these techniques.

Zúñiga and Sánchez (2012) apply an interesting methodology for EDQ to the enrollment of a university in Costa Rica. It deals with the methodology of Arkady Maydanchik (2007) who applied for the analysis of an institutional database carried out in 2011, information of which was evaluated from 1980–2011. An abstract of the methodology is shown in Table 1.1.

On the other hand, Azeroual, Saake and Abuosba (2017) present a methodology related to measurements for data quality and data cleansing for a Research Information System (RIS). According to the authors, the creation of measurements depends on the type of data analyzed: *Laissez faire,* few or rare changes in the nature of the data (errors of incidental nature so they can be ignored); *Reactive approach*, important data and with rare changes (errors are corrected but its causes are not accounted for and it does not need monitoring) and *Proactive approach*, important data that is frequently changed (oriented towards prevention and elimination of the sources of error and tied to constant monitoring). Once a perspective is adopted based

Table 1.1 The Methodology of Arkady Maydanchik

Steps	Description
Collect Data	Both steps are correlated with an exploratory
Data Analysis and Data Tidying	process and with knowledge of the data
Generate Data for Test	Refers to a process to generate new data and different kinds of tests about data
Design of Rules of Data Quality	Refers to the set of restrictions to evaluate data quality
Implementation of Data Quality Rules	Refers to implementation of the rules in code
Adjust the Rules of Data Quality	An iterative process
Tabulation of Aggregate Results	According the preview process it generates tables and aggregate indicators
Dashboard of Data Quality	The result of EDQ is presented in a dashboard

Source: Own elaboration based on Zúñiga & Sánchez (2012: 41).

on the identification of the type of data according to the above, the authors present seven steps for EDQ:

1 Identification of the data to be checked for data quality (typically research-related operational data or data in decision-making reports).
2 Decide which dimensions are used and their weighting.
3 Work out an example of good and bad data for each criterion.
4 Apply the test criterion to the data.
5 Evaluate the test result and whether the quality is acceptable or not.
6 Make corrections where necessary.
7 Repeat the process periodically and observe trends in data quality.

Concomitantly, it is important to remember that nowadays the types of information available on the web include structured and unstructured data, which creates the need to expand the concepts of EDQ. In this sense Hadhiatma (2018) made a revision of the EDQ methods and techniques for Linked Open Data (LOD), whose definition refers to open data at a lower level. This research is important, as it helps us to understand EDQ needs in more complex scenarios such as Big Data, WEB data, WEB semantic, etc. There is evidence that more sophisticated methods are required to identify patterns at a lower level, known as the *"Ontology"* level, where problems of completeness, consistency and precision also tend to occur. That is, the progress in this area is still incipient, since the main problem with the implementation of applications such as Big Data are data quality, data interoperability and data management (Hadhiatma, 2018: 5).

The methodology proposed in this chapter, although it has its encounters with the previous ones, has its differences. They coincide in three key processes at a general level: data exploration, generation of rules or parameters, and evaluation of the results in relation to the parameters and correction. In terms of the added value presented by our methodology, it defines analysis dimensions based on the knowledge of demographic and statistical techniques and does so in a more operational way adapted to the dimensions "data mining" and the "timeline". In addition, the proposed methodology includes a comparison process, which goes beyond the identification of patterns to the construction of standard key indicators where the results can be compared with other data sources. Finally, the methodology is focused on the case of population data, since it makes use of the masculinity index to evaluate the balance of the data sample (although for other areas you can build a simile of a ratio between variables of interest), and uses a theoretical definition of a rate that in mathematical terms represents a frequency of cases in relation to a total. The proposed data source and methodology are detailed below.

1.5 Data and Methodology

This chapter takes as a data source the cases corresponding to the Adult Population Survey (APS) of GEM Colombia (2017), which includes 2098 cases whose methodology and characteristics are explained in detail in Reynolds et al. (2005) (see Table 1.2). The APS considers a set of closed and some open questions for the description of economic activity. The questionnaire starts with filter questions such as age and whether the person is currently trying to start a self-employment business or for an employer. Subsequently, a set of questions is formulated to characterize different aspects of entrepreneurship start-up, business ownership, type of business, reasons for entrepreneurship, source of investment, evaluation of expectations over time, networks, internationalization, potential growth, and support programs for entrepreneurship. There is a control question to identify whether the interviewee is the current owner of an independent business of the declared entrepreneurship. If so, this allows for the registration of other entrepreneurships. Finally, a demographic block is applied in which sex, age, employment, household size, household income, educational level, marital status and socioeconomic status, among others, are considered.

Table 1.2 Distribution of the Adult Population Sample aged 18–64, GEM Colombia Data, 2017

Age Group	2017	Percentage
18–19	115	5.5
20–24	273	13
25–29	270	12.9
30–34	225	10.7
35–39	258	12.3
40–44	206	9.8
45–49	211	10.1
50–54	196	9.3
55–59	179	8.5
60–64	165	7.9
Total	**2,098**	**100**

Source: Own elaboration.

The proposed methodology is based on a value chain that goes from the simplest to the most complex in relation to the number of variables to be considered in order to evaluate the data. The first phase of EDQ begins at the moment the data is available to the user, and involves a set of processes related to the exploration, identification of key variables and in-depth analysis of the behavior of these variables; thus this stage coincides with the definition of "mining data" in the sense that it digs deeply into the data in order to find the "vein", that is to say, the coherence thereof.

Following the value chain set out in Figure 1.1, the simplest indicator to evaluate the behavior of population data in demography is the masculinity index, which is part of the methodology proposed, since it allows us to visualize in a simple way the data distribution under the approximate parameter of 50/50 for the sex ratio. Any behavior that moves away from this standard deserves a thorough evaluation. In addition, since the analysis is performed at individual ages, an analysis of the age declaration can be performed which is susceptible to an incorrect declaration.

Another proposed indicator is the response rates dealing with non-sampling errors (Argote, 2007). The objective is to identify key variables from which to find out whether the population has responded or not responded. Many times, researchers assume that the key variables of their research include data and that they are consistent; however,

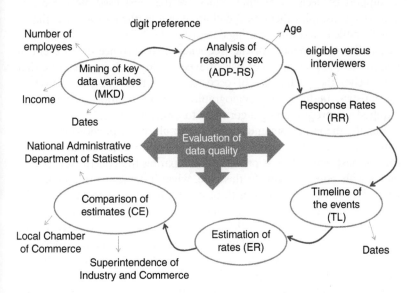

Figure 1.1 The Evaluation of Data Quality (EDQ) Methodology.
Source: Own elaboration.

when doing their analysis, the opposite is true. The response rates, as the name implies, are quotients selected according to the group of interest, and require a knowledge of mathematics and demography for the development of the response tables (see Figure 1.1).

Once you have acceptable response rates or a maximum accepted non-response, the evidence is available to continue with the next EDQ stage. The center of the next stage is "time". This consists of selecting those key variables related to time such as dates, consecutive events, correlated events, etc. in order to perform an analysis of the timeline of the events. This type of variable is often found in demographic and health surveys, which are designed to collect information on women's birth dates. Other longitudinal design studies (e.g., the Mexican National Urban Employment Survey (NUES)) perform the registration of the dates of entry into a new job, with the aim of conducting longitudinal analysis of the individual's history in the labor market. Likewise, the registration of dates allows for survival analysis. This analysis allows for the verification of the consistency with which the events were declared and for the identification of anomalies.

The following process responds to more complex mathematical concepts from the point of view of demography and the probability theory, since the aim is to create measurements of social phenomena (indicators) in support of decision making. Rates are the most used measurements and have a complex theoretical definition in a mathematical sense that is usually difficult to estimate using dates (Argote, 2007, 2009). The aim of a rate is the measurement of the frequency of occurrence of an event in relation to the population at risk of experiencing it. It is a measure that approaches the probability of occurrence. At this stage, a knowledge of statistics, mathematics, demography and information technology is required for programming algorithms to estimate a rate.

Finally, the indicators and charts, the result of the previous processes, constitute a set of measurements obtained from the data source, the input for the next stage. It is a process of comparing the consistency of estimates with other sources. In this case, when it comes to rate indicators defined as standard such as birth or death rates, if two sources have the same measure the comparison is feasible. For non-traditional measurements it is necessary to apply the same methodology for the sources to be compared or to otherwise find approximations, so that the consistency of estimates can be evaluated (as Argote did in 2018) to compare different estimates of the Mexican population projection (Argote, 2015).

The previous summarized explanation of the methodology is detailed below in terms of the procedure and mathematical formulation in the case of the APS GEM data.

1.5.1 Mining of Key Data Variables (MKD)

This first phase consists in exploring the variables, knowing and identifying them both in the instruments for their collection and in the database to which they must correspond (see Table 1.3). Mining implies the following procedures:

- Revision of the names of the variables, labels and their categories in the database for the user's understanding.
- Analyze and execute frequency commands of demographic variables (sex, age, marital status, income level, educational level, etc.), variables that allow us to know the population or sample under study. This data must be consistent with similar samples or with other data sources.

This stage implies carrying out the following procedures in a database processing program (SPSS, STATA, TABLEAU):

- Recode variables for easy location. In big databases the location of the variables is difficult, and in order to maintain the premise of not modifying the original database it is recommended to copy the variables of interest in others that are located at the end of the database for quick location.
- Recategorize variables to standardize. For those cases in which variables have multiple categories such as economic activity or simple ages, it is recommended to recode to simplify the number of categories according to such standards as international codes, five-year age groups, etc.
- Variable crossing allows us to evaluate the coherence between variables. It is important to carry out crossing of variables such as age versus sex, as it allows us to observe the coherence of the data distribution. Regarding entrepreneurship with APS GEM, it is interesting to cross the variables of the current number of employees versus the expected number of employees in the next five years, as it allows us to identify anomalies.

1.5.2 Analysis of Digit Preference and Reason by Sex (ADP-RS)

The analysis of the data by individual ages allows us to evaluate the digit preference in the declaration of age, and its distribution by sex allows us to construct the masculinity index to evaluate the distribution by sex of the data. These two demographic variables, namely sex and

Table 1.3 Key Variables on Entrepreneurship, APS GEM

Key Questions (Variables)	Description
bstart	Q1A1. Are you, alone or with others, currently trying to start a new business, including any self-employment or selling any goods or services to others?
bjobst	Q1A2. Are you, alone or with others, currently trying to start a new business or a new venture for your employer as part of your normal work?
suacts	Q1B. Over the past 12 months have you done anything to help start this new business?
subustype	Q1F. What kind of business is this?
sunowjob	Q1H1. Not counting the owners, how many people are currently working for this business?
suyr5job	Q1H2. Not counting owners, how many people will be working for this business five years from now?
ownmge	Q2A. Are you, alone or with others, currently the owner of a business you help manage, self-employed, or selling any goods or services to others?
ombustype	Q2F. What kind of business is this?
futsup	Q3A. Are you, alone or with others, expecting to start a new business, including any type of self-employment, within the next three years?
discent	Q3B. Have you, in the past 12 months, sold, shut down, discontinued or quit a business you owned and managed, any form of self-employment, or selling goods or services to anyone?
Demographic Variables	
Gender	A. What is your gender?
Age	B. What is your current age (in years)?
hhsize	E. How many members make up your permanent household, including you?
cohhinc	F. Which of these ranges best describes the total annual income of all the members of your household, including your income, as one combined figure?
coreduc	G. What is the highest level of education you have completed?
costrata	M. Survey vendor to indicate stratum which corresponds to the respondent, if applicable to sample.
dtsurv	N. Date of survey (dd.mm.yy).

Source: Own elaboration.

age, are determinant variables of many social behaviors and tend to carry considerable weight in most mathematical models designed to explain population behavior.

The masculinity index is the ratio between the number of men at age x and the number of women at the same age. This is the reason that measures the number of men per 100 women.

$$IM = \frac{H_x}{M_x}$$

(1)

The reason it is an indicator for EDQ is because there are parameters for the behavior of the reason by sex and this allows for the evaluation of how large a gap there is between the behavior of the data samples in relation with the parameters. In this case, the ratio is expected to be close to one for all ages.

In Figure 1.1 we observed the behavior of IM for the 2017 Colombia GEM data. The behavior of the curve is erratic according to the individual ages; a pattern cannot be distinguished and it is striking that the approximated 50/50 rule applies in only a few cases; that is to say, close to 1. This shows us that the characteristics of the sample are unique features. On the contrary, GEM methodology does not take into account age and sex intervals for select APS samples, which can present imbalances, as observed in Figure 1.2.

The revision of the age declaration is relevant to EDQ because it is an indicator of the consistency of the data. According to several demographic studies (e.g., Pressat, 2000), there is a preference for declaring even numbers or those ending in zero. These are cases where people declare a younger age, among others. Therefore, by looking at individual ages, we can observe whether there are patterns that are not consistent.

1.5.3 Response Rates (RR)

The idea of response rates is to calculate the percentage of people eligible to answer a question, and who really answered. The response rates are expected to be very close to 100 percent because it tells us how the population responded. Response is understood to be that which is in the range of possible answers that are different to non-responding (NR) or lost data (MISSING).

For the estimation of response rates, matrices are constructed to allow for the calculation of reasons. The matrices represent group and subgroup arrangements according to five-year age groups, which by convention is the pattern to organizing population data. The simplest

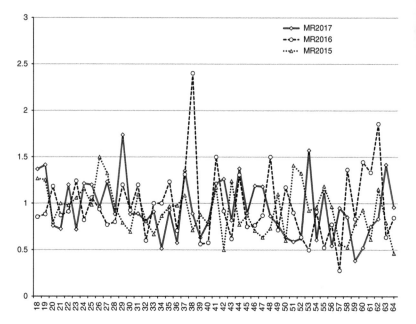

Figure 1.2 Masculinity Rate, GEM Colombia Data, 2017.

Source: Own elaboration using GEM data.

matrix is the distribution of the total population by five-year age groups (denominators of rates).

For the calculation of subgroups that make up the possible numerators, filters are used to select the cases that have an answer. In this sense, the question to be evaluated is selected in advance; for example, in the GEM case, we have control questions: Have you started an entrepreneurship in the past 12 months? (YES/NO). The response rate for this variable has as a numerator the number of cases that answered "Yes" between the total population of that age group (See Table 1.4).

$$TR = \frac{Answers_{x+5}}{Eligibles_{x+5}} \tag{2}$$

1.5.4 Timeline of the Events (TL)

Time is one of the key variables in statistics and demography. From a statistical point of view, the entities under study – in this case the

Table 1.4 Entrepreneurship Response Rates, GEM Colombia Data, 2017

Age	Women				Men			
	Total Women in the Sample	Eligible	Respondent	Answer Rate	Total Men in the Sample	Eligible	Respondent	Answer Rate
18–19	48	9	7	77.8	70	20	15	75
20–24	142	42	30	71.4	125	40	26	65
25–29	139	39	28	71.8	154	38	26	68.4
30–34	127	38	24	63.2	108	35	21	60
35–39	139	50	29	58	116	32	20	62.5
40–44	100	25	16	64	100	31	22	71
45–49	107	30	24	80	97	30	14	46.7
50–54	114	40	25	62.5	93	24	13	54.2
55–59	90	16	7	43.8	79	31	16	51.6
60–64	86	12	7	58.3	64	17	10	58.8
Total	**1,092**	**301**	**197**	**65.4**	**1,006**	**298**	**183**	**61.4**

Source: Own elaboration using data from APS GEM.

population or the companies – are not static entities but exhibit a behavior over time. Therefore, when modeling real phenomena, it is crucial to have a record of the time.

Unfortunately, not all cases have a record of dates that correspond to the events we wish to study. In these cases it is feasible to perform an analysis of the sequence of events, since some events precede others. For example, in the case of fertility, individuals are first born before entering school, but if this sequence is detected upside down it is an anomaly. In the case of entrepreneurship, the idea of entrepreneurship is expected to be followed by formal registration and so on. If questions about this process exist, it is feasible to evaluate a timeline of events.

The starting point for the sequence of events with or without a date is the bivariate analysis between consecutive events (variables). In this way it is possible to construct variable crossing tables to evaluate inconsistencies that may arise in this regard. For the sequence analysis of more variables there are more sophisticated methods such as life trajectory analysis or survival analysis that are used in longitudinal studies.

In the case of entrepreneurship with 2017 GEM Colombia data, a table is constructed by five-year age groups in which the number of people who claim to be undertaking an entrepreneurship (bstart), the number of people who take any action on their entrepreneurship are recorded (suacts), then if you declare that at the time of the interview you own a business (ownmge), and finally those who respond that they closed a business (discent) (see Table 1.5).

1.5.5 Estimation of Rates (ER)

Estimating a rate is not a simple exercise. The definition of different demographic measures tells us about it. According to Moreno, López, and Corcho (2000), the rate, comprising a number and denominator, is a type of quotient among others (detailed in Chapter 2, this volume) which represents the methodology for estimating the Global Entrepreneurship Rate. According to the above, a theoretical rate is defined as follows:

$$Rate = \frac{Number\ of\ events\ which\ occur\ in\ a\ determined\ period\ of\ time}{Exposition\ time\ of\ the\ individuals\ until\ they\ experiment\ the\ event}$$

As an example, the Global Fertility Rate is defined as standard worldwide and whose calculation is carried out as follows:

$$GFT = \frac{Number\ of\ births\ per\ woman}{Time\ of\ exposure\ x_i}$$

Table 1.5 Timeline of Entrepreneurship Events, GEM Colombia Data, 2017

Edad	Women					Men				
	Total Women in the Sample	Eligible		Respondent		Total Men in the Sample	Eligible		Respondent	
		Bstart	Suacts	Ownrge	Discent		Bstart	Suacts	Ownrge	Discent
		Start a Business	Do an Action of Their Undertaking	Owner	Close Business		Start a Business	Do an Action of Their Undertaking	Owner	Close Business
18–19	48	9	7	5	0	70	20	15	9	4
20–24	142	42	30	28	7	125	40	26	23	5
25–29	139	39	28	25	10	154	38	26	21	9
30–34	127	38	24	30	8	108	35	21	18	8
35–39	139	50	29	36	5	116	32	20	26	7
40–44	100	25	16	20	7	100	31	22	26	6
45–49	107	30	24	27	3	97	30	14	28	11
50–54	114	40	25	28	8	93	24	13	31	10
55–59	90	16	7	14	7	79	31	16	29	7
60–64	86	12	7	10	4	64	17	10	14	7
Total	**1,092**	**301**	**197**	**223**	**59**	**1,006**	**298**	**183**	**225**	**74**

Source: Own elaboration.

Being the denominator the time of exposure is from the age of 18 up until the birth event experience (in the reproductive age period for a woman, i.e., aged 18–45).

In the case of entrepreneurship (see Chapter 2), the global entrepreneurship rate is defined as follows:

$$GET = \frac{Number\ of\ undertakings}{Exposure\ time\ to\ experience\ an\ event}$$

This is where the exposure time is the time that elapses from the age of 18 up to the moment of undertaking an enterprise in the productive age (aged 18–64). The exposure time is measured in person years (Pressat, 2000). However, if there is no data on dates, by convention the population of the mid-term age group is taken as an average (see details in Chapter 2).

The Global Entrepreneurship Rate (GER) calculations for the case of Colombia using GEM 2017 data are presented in Table 1.6. A rate of 2,053 ventures is estimated in the productive life of an adult under the assumption of constant risk undertaken. Table 1.6 and Figure 1.3 also show the specific rates of entrepreneurship that integrate the GER, which allow for measuring entrepreneurship by five-year age groups at rates per 1,000 adults.

1.5.6 Comparison of Estimates (CE)

The construction of indicators is a key part of EDQ; however, it is important to compare the results with other sources in order to validate them. In this sense, this phase requires expert knowledge of the subject of the data source in order to be aware of other sources of information with useful data to construct similar indicators that allow for comparison.

Concerning entrepreneurship in Colombia, there are several sources of information. The search for data on the subject begins at national level with official institutions such as DANE[1] and CCB[2] and at the international level with institutions such as The World Bank, Euromonitor, GEM, Doing Business, etc.

The comparison requires official sources that have the required data. In the case of Colombia, the official data source at individual level is owned by the DANE institution which carried out many surveys and aggregated data population related to employment and unemployment at national level in 2017 through the Great Integrated Household Survey (GIHS) and data from the micro-business module of 2015. The data of the EAP[3] in the first semester of 2017 is taken as denominator and as numerator the amount of micro-businesses of the GIHS of the

Table 1.6 Specific Entrepreneurship Rates and GER by Five-year Age Groups

Five-Year Age Groups	Total			
	Total Population	Do an Action of Their Undertaking	Specific Annual Rate	Rates by 1,000
18–19	118	22	0.093	93.22
20–24	267	56	0.042	41.948
25–29	293	54	0.037	36.86
30–34	235	45	0.038	38.298
35–39	255	49	0.038	38.431
40–44	200	38	0.038	38
45–49	204	38	0.037	37.255
50–54	207	38	0.037	36.715
55–59	169	23	0.027	27.219
60–64	150	17	0.023	22.667
Total	**2,098**	**380**	**0.411**	
Global Entrepreneurship Rate:			2.053	

Source: Own elaboration.

Note: The first group is not a five-year age group because the APS interviews adults aged 18–64, but the method adjusts the two years of this group.

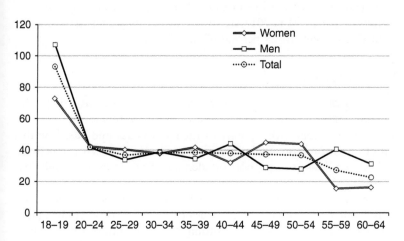

Figure 1.3 Specific Entrepreneurship Rates per Five-year Age Groups, GEM Colombia Data, 2017.

Source: Own elaboration.

Table 1.7 Estimation of the Proportion of Entrepreneurships in Colombia, 2017

Numerator	2015	EAP 2017	PEP
Total Number of Small Enterprises	4,662	24,581	18.97
Total Number of Small Enterprises of Employer	603	24,581	2.45
Total Number of Small Enterprises of Self-Employer	4,059	24,581	16.51

Source: Own elaboration.

Notes:
The source of the data for 2015 is the Big Survey Integrated of Homes of Colombia. The EAP was taken from the National Department Administrative of Statistics of Colombia, 2017.
EAP: Economically Active Population
PEP: Percentage of Entrepreneurship Population.

2015 national total, information of which is available. It is possible to adopt this approach, since there is no national data source similar to that collected by GEM Colombia.

As can be seen in Table 1.7, an approach to the Entrepreneurial Activity Rate (EAR) defined by the GEM is estimated to mean *Total Early Entrepreneurship Activity (TEA)* (see Chapter 2, this volume) which in this case takes as denominator the economically active population in Colombia in the first half of 2017 and as numerator the amount of micro-businesses of the 2016 total national GIHS for an EAR of 18.97 percent of enterprises in Colombia. The EAR of Colombia, according to the GEM in 2017, decreased significantly compared to 2016, from 27.6 percent to18.9 percent (GEM, 2017).

1.6 Conclusions

EDQ is a phase of data science which is not simple, but it is fundamental. An EDQ methodology allows us to formulate the scientific argument to support the quality of the source data and based on this data to perform more sophisticated processes such as DA predictions, and AI simulations in support of adequate decision making and close to reality (Argote, 2015).

EDQ is a thorough process of identifying patterns and anomalies. This chapter has presented techniques from engineering, mathematics, demography and statistics. According to the literature review, there are general processes that are part of EDQ; however, the proposed methodology follows a value chain from the simple to the complex that allows for concrete results to be obtained in a practical way.

The proposed methodology, unlike the revised ones, emphasizes the estimation of rates, analysis of the timelines and comparison of the results with other data sources, which guarantees the valuation of coherence, validity and quality of the data considering both sampling and non-sampling errors. The methodology is available to all audiences, since it makes use of instruments such as tables, matrices and Excel and the SPSS for data registration.

Notes

1 National Administrative Department of Statistics.
2 Bogotá Chamber of Commerce.
3 Economically Active Population (EAP).

References

Argote Cusi, M. (2003). Evaluación de la calidad del dato. In Estimación de la distribución estadística de la Tasa Global de Fecundidad mediante remuestreo, retrieved from: http://conocimientoabierto.flacso.edu.mx/tesis/103.

Argote Cusi, M. (2007). Estimación de la distribución estadística de la Tasa Global de Fecundidad. *Papeles de Población*, 54(13), 87–113.

Argote Cusi, M. (2009). Comparación y evaluación de la distribución estadística del estimador de la tasa global de fecundidad de Bolivia en 1998 y 2003. *Papeles de Población*, 62(15), 201–222.

Argote Cusi, M. (2015). Sensitivity analysis of projections population. *Papeles de Población*, 84(21), 45–67.

Argote-Cusi, M. L. (2018). El uso de lógica difusa en proyecciones de población: el caso de México. *Papeles de población*, 24(95), 273–301.

Azeroual, O., Saake, G. & Abuosba, M. (2019). Data quality measures and data cleansing for research information systems. *arXiv preprint* arXiv:1901.06208.

Hadhiatma, A. (2018). Improving data quality in the linked open data: A survey. *Journal of Physics: Conference Series*, 978(1), 012026.

Heredia, R., Jobany, J. & Vilalta Alonso, J. A. (2009). La calidad de los datos: su importancia para la gestión empresarial. *Libre Empresa*, 6(1), 43–50.

Maydanchik, A. (2007). *Data Quality Assessment*. Technics Publications, Basking Ridge, NJ.

Moreno-Altamirano, A., López-Moreno, S. & Corcho-Berdugo, A. (2000). Principales medidas en epidemiología. *Salud pública de México*, 42, 337–348.

Pressat, R. (2000). *El análisis demográfico: Métodos, resultados, aplicaciones*. Fondo de cultura Económica, Mexico City.

Reynolds, P., Bosma, N., Autio, E., Hunt, S., De Bono, N., Servais, I. & Chin, N. (2005). *Global Entrepreneurship Monitor: Design and Implementation 1998–2003* (No. 1101). Global Entrepreneurship Research Association.

Zúñiga Segura, L. & Sánchez Godínez, E. (2012). Calidad de datos y su evaluación: un caso de estudio. *Calidad en la Educación Superior*, 3(2), 33–49.

2 The Global Entrepreneurship Rate

A Methodological Proposal

It is wonderful to see how numbers express the language of the universe.

2.1 Introduction

Ian Steward states in his book on the history of mathematics that over the past 10,000 years the measurement of social phenomena has been of constant interest. Some of the most interesting examples of measurements are the earth's size and age, speed of light, value of π, etc., estimates that have been made using different methods and techniques and that have led to scientific advances in mathematics, probabilities and engineering (Stewart, 2007: 40).

In particular, the economy is a science that contains many techniques to measure social phenomena, a science whose paradigms and main postulates are supported by modeling mathematical tools and the construction of metrics that make it possible to measure and model the economic dynamics and its variables (Akerlof & Shiller, 2016). Demography, centered on populations, has a theoretical-mathematical apparatus convergent with probability and statistics for the construction of basic input indicators for resource planning in nations. Various country indicators make use of population as the denominator of national statistics, even for the distribution of public resources (Pressat, 2000; Preston, Heuveline & Guillot, 2001; Rowland, 2003; Siegel & Swanson, 2004; Gut, 2013).

The study of entrepreneurship as a social object is no different from the previous context of measurement, and in this respect global projects such as the Global Entrepreneurship Monitor (GEM) which collect two surveys with statistical representation in each country, one oriented to the adult population aged 18–64, and the other focused on entrepreneurship ecosystem experts that measure entrepreneurial activity in each country and allow the characterization of the profiles of entrepreneurs (Goméz et al., 2018; GEM, 2017, 2018; Argote & Parra, 2018). Other projects such as the Global Entrepreneurship Index (GEI) and the Systematic Conditions Index (SCI) are aimed at measuring the level of development and maturation of the entrepreneurial ecosystem as well as the availability of infrastructure and macroeconomic strength to generate dynamic companies (Acs, Autio & Szerb, 2014; Kantis, Federico & Menéndez, 2012). The results of these projects are widely affected by the demographic structure of the countries from which they collect the information, thus requiring the innovation and production of new metrics in order to improve the quality of measurements carried out.

According to the above, the objective of this chapter is to present a methodological proposal for the calculation of a rate for the measurement of entrepreneurship. It should be noted that entrepreneurship is an issue that has gained worldwide importance in recent years, since there is theoretical evidence of its positive effects on economic development, which is why many countries have adopted public policies to support entrepreneurship programs (Audretsch, Kuratko & Link, 2016: 11; Acs & Szerb, 2007; Astebro & Robinson, 2016: 37–40; Akerlof & Shiller, 2016: 214–223).

The methodological proposal is presented as follows. First, mathematical theoretical support is given in the construction of a rate as a measure that absorbs the complexity of the phenomenon. Second, the mathematical definitions of Specific Rates and Global Rates are presented. In a third section the previous mathematical model is contextualized to highlight the current importance of entrepreneurship as an economic phenomenon of populations, the state of the art of their measurement and the sources of data currently available. The fourth section focuses on the description of the data and the methodology applied to entrepreneurship. The fifth section presents the results of the different estimates of Specific Entrepreneurship Rate (SER) and Global Entrepreneurship Rate (GER) for the Colombian data series between 2008–2017. Finally, a discussion of the results and conclusions is presented.

2.2 The Measurement of Social Phenomena

According to Moreno, López and Corcho (2000: 337), measurement is an indispensable procedure in scientific practice. Scientific research is born out of the observation of the phenomenon included in a research question that relates to a set of independent variables that explain the dependent variable. The tip of the iceberg is the operationalization of the null hypothesis that we must contrast to conclude in a scientific way whether our statements are true or false. It is at this point that the measurement of the variables that make up the hypothesis is a crucial process for the successful completion of any scientific research.

Measurement consists of a value to the characteristic or attribute of a variable; therefore measurement is a process of abstraction of the step from a theoretical entity to a conceptual scale and then to an operational scale. For example, in entrepreneurship the entrepreneur is not measured as such, but rather for one of his or her characteristics such as age, type of undertaking, sex, etc. Measurement is also a process of comparison with other values to evaluate changes over time. Moreno et al. (2000) set out clearly the steps for measurement: (1) the part of the event to be measured is defined, (2) the scale with which it will be measured is selected, (3) the measured attribute is compared with the scale, and finally (4) a judgment of value is issued about the results of the comparison.

To measure entrepreneurship, for example, first, the variables to be measured are selected (age, sex, number of employees, seniority), and second, the measurement scales are selected (completed years, male or female, persons, years of entrepreneurship). Then the attributes are compared with the selected scales (30 years, woman, ten employees, three years) and finally a judgment of value is issued, as a result of comparing the data found, with certain standards as to the specific characteristics of the entrepreneurship, to determine whether the entrepreneurship is dynamic or not (Audretsch et al., 2016; Kantis et al., 2012).

It is from the position of these fundamental mathematical concepts of probabilities and statistics that the concepts and definitions of demographic analysis are addressed for the theoretical definition of a "rate" and, in this case, as a measure of the dynamics of entrepreneurship.

2.3 Demographic Measures

The mathematical fundament developed by demography for the study of population is applicable to different areas, since the population variable is crucial to many mathematical models that seek to explain the behavior of social systems.

The study of population acquires scientific and objective character by algebraically representing and managing population data. The first mathematical instrument for the representation of populations is a table with data of population in a given year. It is not by chance that Pressat (2000) in his book on demographic analysis starts with a mortality table constructed from a series of data from mortality registers of the French population of 1820. In equation (1) we can see that x is the succession of anniversaries that take the values 0, 1, 2, 3 … 100; the deaths $d(x, x + 1)$

where x is the first anniversary and $x + 1$ the following anniversary; the survivors S_x after one year, two years, three years ... 100 years and a more elaborate notion, the mortality ratio defined as follows:

$$q_x = \frac{d(x, x + 1)}{S_x} \tag{1}$$

where q_x is the mortality ratio that statistically evaluates the risk involved on a given anniversary death before the next anniversary. Tables of marriage, fertility, migration and interaction of these variables can be constructed in the same way, as can be seen in Pressat (2000: 17). Making use of deduction, these data series and their relationship to each other are actually capable of being represented by a data distribution function, which is a mathematical model of the phenomenon under study generated from the data table (see the survivor curves, death, etc. in Pressat (2000: 17)).

One of the essential variables of demography is time. The events that happen to a population are carried out over time. For this reason, the demographic analysis develops several instruments to represent time in the mathematical modeling of the phenomena. For example, the lexis diagram allows the representation of time on a coordinate axis (x), age in years (y), the cohort of populations that go through time and the events they experience (see Figure 2.1).

The position or location of the event over time is very important in demography. Thus, in demography we study the number of births per woman, the number of deaths per year, the number of migrants per year, etc. For the present case we study the number of entrepreneurships in a year. We can see the events–time relationship of the previous examples.

Considering the significance of time in demography, it is important to define the variable duration. Because timing of the event is crucial in the demographic analysis, the mathematical representation of time was necessary in the lexis diagram (Figure 2.1). The idea behind the diagram is to represent the events in time related to the age at which they occur. Figure 2.2 shows the exact duration and duration in years of age of an individual, "M". Between one and two years the point "M" is greater than 1 and closer to 2 but we do not know *a priori* the exact age, in months, days, hours, etc. Therefore, the concept of duration, in these terms, is a segment of the timeline whose calculations can be very precise according to the availability of information (in the case of entrepreneurship it is feasible to place the entrepreneur on the timeline, the moment at which he becomes an entrepreneur and later related events).

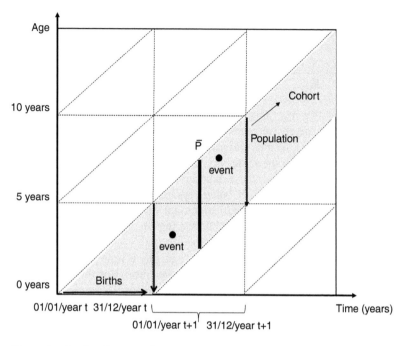

Figure 2.1 Lexis Diagram of a Rate.

Source: Own elaboration.

Note: The Lexis diagram represents the dynamic of population; the rate has been defined as the number of the event in a period of time between the number of population exposure to the event.

The above derives from the concept of "years–person" and the concept of rate that we will discuss in detail in the following section. The demographic events are quantified during a specific period of time, generally one year, and the complexity of the rate lies in the relationship between the events and the effect on that population in which they occur. *A priori*, the population is a variable that changes over a year, due to the inflows and outflows of the population, for which there is uncertainty in terms of the population that must appear in the denomination of a rate. Faced with this situation, demography defines that the sum of time in which the population has remained to which the events occurred during the year of observation, measured in the concept of "years–person" and figures as denominator in the theoretical definition of a rate, as long as it can be calculated (because it requires date data of events, information that is not always available).

(a)

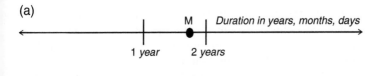

(b)

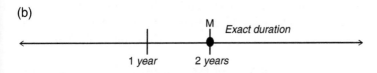

Figure 2.2 Exact Duration and Duration in Years.
Source: Own elaboration.

2.4 The Rate: Indicator Summary

A rate is a quotient widely used in demographic analysis and other disciplines. Its quality lies in representing summarized information which is represented in tables (Pressat, 2000: 104). There are two types of rates: those that relate the incidents or events to the population at risk of experiencing them, or those that relate sub-populations to populations; the first are those that present the most complex mathematical abstractions and are more accurately denominated as "theoretical rates" (Argote, 2007), since the estimate requires specific information on durations (dates).

The rate is one type of quotient among others.

Proportions

> Proportions are measures that express the frequency with which an event occurs in relation to the total population in which it may occur. This measure is calculated by dividing the number of events that occurred between the populations in which they occurred.
>
> (Moreno et al., 2000: 339)

Reasons

> The reasons can be defined as magnitudes that express the existing arithmetic relationship between two events, in the same population or one single event in two populations.
>
> (Moreno et al., 2000: 340)

Rates

> Rates express the dynamics of an event in a population over time. They can be defined as the magnitude of the change of one variable (illness or death) per unit of change (usually time) in relation to the size of the population that is at risk of experiencing the event. Unlike a proportion, the denominator of a rate does not express the number of subjects under observation but rather the time during which such subjects were at risk of suffering the event.
>
> (Moreno et al., 2000: 339)

Rate is the quotient of a set of events between the exposure times that the people live to experiment the event. The duration of exposure time is measured in the "years–person" lived during the period of observation. When there is no information on duration, the population is used as the denominator in the middle of the time interval as an approximation to the number of "years–person" lived under the assumption of homogeneity of distribution of events over time (Argote, 2003, 2007).

An example of the estimation of theoretical rate can be seen in Argote (2007), with information about the date of birth of children to Bolivian women in a retrospective survey on fertility, which is the theoretical empirical fundament for this article. This algorithm is taken into account for the calculation of the numerator and denominator of the proposed Global Entrepreneurship Rate.

For subsequent inferences it is important to answer the following question: Is the concept of rate and probability the same? The hard data itself does not tell us much about decision making, and that is why quotients provide more information by relating events with the population to which it happens, which is an approximation to the risk (Pressat, 2000; Argote, 2003, 2007). Based on this, a probability is similar to a rate except that the denominator of a probability involves all the people in a population from "the start" of the observation period, while a rate takes the population "in the middle" of the period. That is to say, a rate is a measure that is able to capture the risk and probability of the event under study (Gut, 2013).

2.5 Why Measure Entrepreneurship?

Entrepreneurship as an object of study has been a topic of great relevance for the social sciences and in particular for the economy since the initial proposals of Richard Cantillon's classical theory in 1700, which defined the entrepreneur as a crucial player in the balance of the economy, because he was the one in charge of redistributing income and multiplying the generated wealth. Centuries later Schumpeter awards the entrepreneur a leading role in the economy by indicating that his main function is to reform and revolutionize the forms of production through the use of invention, which in turn would generate a process of creative destruction in the business fabric of the economies that would promote the development and growth of more dynamic and innovative productive units (Cantillon, 1755; Schumpeter, 1934; Audretsch, Kuratko & Link, 2016; Acs & Szerb, 2007; Astebro & Robinson, 2016: 37–40; Akerlof & Shiller, 2016: 214–223; Parra & Argote, 2013).

Nowadays, several global research projects have focused their attention on the study of entrepreneurship as a driving force in the economy (Audretsch et al., 2016; Parra & Argote, 2017). The Global Entrepreneurship Monitor, for example, focuses on measuring the business activity of countries in differentiating the types of entrepreneurships generated in an economy from among those oriented by necessity which are created in the absence of other income resources or job opportunities for individuals, and those oriented by opportunity which subjects choose to undertake as a mechanism to increase their income, job independence or to take advantage of a market opportunity (Gómez et al., 2018; GEM, 2017; Argote & Parra, 2018).

The measurement of entrepreneurship generated in an economy is essential to the design and execution of public policies aimed at strengthening the entrepreneurship ecosystem and readjusts strategically the public funds for production and public development of a nation (Gómez et al., 2018; Parra & Argote, 2017). In this context entrepreneurial metrics are very useful both for academics and decision makers when identifying the percentage of the economically active population that sees in entrepreneurship a life and work development option as opposed to the occupied population employed as wage-earning or unpaid workers (Parra & Argote, 2018).

Taking into account the above, the GEM project created the TEA (Total Early Entrepreneurial Activity) indicator that measures the proportion of adults aged 18–64 who have been involved in the implementation of a new business or entrepreneurship in the past 12 months, either personally of within the company for which they work (Gómez et al., 2018). The TEA is not an entrepreneurial rate in a strict sense, given that it is calculated from a proportion, which allows for the establishment of a percentage of the population of working age that have been involved in an entrepreneurial initiative during the past year (Entrepreneurship Research Conference, 2017).

The other global project that measures the conditions and systematic factors associated with entrepreneurship is the Global Entrepreneurship Index (GEI), which takes as reference seven analytical dimensions from which the level of favorability of the conditions of the macro environments in a nation are analyzed so that new entrepreneurships are generated, mainly of a dynamic nature. These dimensions are the structure of the market, the availability of infrastructure, science and technology systems, access and soundness of the financial sector, the educational system, government programs aimed at entrepreneurial development and the stoutness of the private sector (Acs, Szerb & Lloyd, 2018). In relation to this indicator, it can be observed that although GEI generates measurements at a systematic level which are necessary to understand if a country or region has the conditions and a favorable environment, it does not allow for the analysis of the characterization of entrepreneurship at an individual level, their frequency with regard to age intervals, gender or educational level, which is possible when analyzing an adult population survey (APS) carried out by the GEM globally, and that has representation at country level in each of the nations in which it is implemented every year.

Unlike the previous chapter, this chapter details a new proposal for the measurement: the Global Entrepreneurship Rate (GER) for a country which can be separated by age intervals and interpreted for each 1,000 individuals of productive age. The proposed GER, rather than pretending to be a substitute for the indicators currently produced in the area of entrepreneurship such as TEA and GEI, will be considered to complement them.

2.6 Data

The *Global Entrepreneurship Monitor* (GEM) has collected information on entrepreneurship in approximately 100 countries every year since 1999 by means of two types of survey: the *Adult Population Survey* (APS) and the *National Expert Survey* (NES) at both individual and national levels. The conceptual model and the dimensions taken into account in the surveys are given in detail in Reynolds et al. (2005: 212).

The current research takes as a data source the APS Colombia between 2008–2017, available online for the universities that form part of the GEM consortium. The APS considers a set of closed and some open questions for a description of economic activity. The questionnaire begins with filter questions such as age and whether the person is currently trying to start up a business for self-employment or for an employer. Subsequently, a set of questions are formulated to characterize different aspects of entrepreneurship start-up, ownership of the business, type of business, reasons for the undertaking, the source of the investment, evaluation of expectations over time, networks, internationalization, growth potential, support programs and training for entrepreneurship. There is a control question to identify whether the person interviewed is the current owner of an independent business, of the declared undertaking, and, if so, this enables the registration of other entrepreneurships. Finally, a demographic segment is applied which considers sex, age, employment, household size, household income, educational level, marital status and socioeconomic strata, among others.

Table 2.1 shows the distribution of the series of cases interviewed by the GEM project in Colombia for five-year age groups and their percentage of participation in the annual sample. It can be observed that the total of the sample increased considerably between 2010–2011 (See Figure 2.3), while for the other years it remained at between 2,000 and 4,000 cases. This is due to the fact that during those years, in addition to the national sample, regional samples were added. The percentage of participation by age groups in each data sample is very similar for all years, namely between 12 and 13 percent participation between the groups 20–24, 25–29, 30–34, 35–39 and 40–44, which correspond to the productive age of the adult population, between 6 and 7 percent in the youngest (18–19) group and also a low percentage for the adult-older ages of around 9 percent for the 50–54 group and around 7 percent for the 55–59 and 60–64 groups.

2.7 Method

According to the state-of-the art demography discussed in sections 2.3 and 4 it is essential to begin with the theoretical definition of a rate. Rate is the quotient of the number of events that occurred (numerator) between the exposure times of the people to experiment the event (denominator) measured in "years–person":

$$\text{Rate} = \frac{\textit{Number of events}_{x,x+1}^{t,t+1}}{\textit{Time of exposure}_{x,x+1}^{t,t+1}} \tag{2}$$

In the case of entrepreneurship, the numerator is the number of undertakings in time t, t + 1 and group of age $x, x + 1$, and the denominator is the exposure time of adults to experience the event, which in this case is

Table 2.1 GEM Data Sample, APS Colombia, 2008–2017

Age Group	2008	(%)	2009	(%)	2010	(%)	2011	(%)	2012	(%)	2013	(%)	2014	(%)	2015	(%)	2016	(%)	2017	(%)
18–19	124	6	299	7.4	701	6.4	718	6.9	409	6.3	216	6.4	251	6.8	242	6.6	140	6.8	115	5.5
20–24	258	13	569	14	1,441	13.1	1,466	14.1	920	14.2	485	14.3	493	13.4	446	12.1	362	17.5	273	13
25–29	231	12	485	12	1,221	11.1	1,276	12.3	913	14.1	428	12.6	416	11.3	462	12.6	263	12.7	270	12.9
30–34	235	12	466	11.5	1,219	11.1	1,206	11.6	902	13.9	418	12.3	455	12.3	446	12.1	229	11.1	225	10.7
35–39	247	12	431	10.6	1,112	10.1	1,078	10.4	717	11.1	343	10.1	406	11	426	11.6	221	10.7	258	12.3
40–44	225	11	471	11.6	1,267	11.5	1,153	11.1	874	13.5	371	10.9	387	10.5	386	10.5	186	9	206	9.8
45–49	243	12	411	10.1	1,213	11	1,046	10.1	504	7.8	330	9.7	372	10.1	362	9.8	176	8.5	211	10.1
50–54	176	9	353	8.7	1,112	10.1	1,014	9.8	535	8.3	339	10	385	10.4	398	10.8	189	9.1	196	9.3
55–59	140	7	288	7.1	916	8.3	752	7.2	362	5.6	229	6.7	260	7	362	7.1	174	8.4	179	8.5
60–64	121	6	280	6.9	827	7.5	665	6.4	335	5.2	241	7.1	266	7.2	253	6.9	127	6.1	165	7.9
Total cases	2,000	100	4,053	100	11,029	100	10,374	100	6,471	100	3,400	100	3,691	100	3,681	100	2,067	100	2,098	100

Source: Own calculation using information from www.gemconsortium.org.

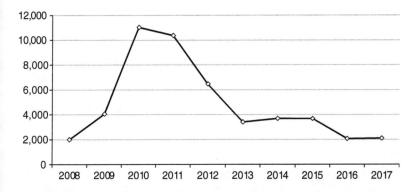

Figure 2.3 Number of Cases in the APS Colombia, 2008–2017.

Source: Own calculations using the APS database 2008–2017 for Colombia.

to undertake or start a business of self-employment or for an employer. In this way we define a measure that relates the number of entrepreneurships with the adult population to obtain a measure of the frequency of the event in the population. The methodologically more complicated aspect of the calculation is the denominator, since it is "duration" (Argote, 2007), and requires a data source with dates, information the APS does not have, so the total number of the adult population interviewed is taken from the specific age group as a proxy of the theoretical denominator.

Thus, taking the previous theoretical support, the Global Entrepreneurship Rate (GER) is defined as the summary of the linear combination of the Specific Entrepreneurship Rates (SER) multiplied by five, constants that correspond to the five-year group:

$$SER_{x,x+5}^{t,t+1} = \frac{Entrepreneurship_{x,x+5}^{t,t+1}}{Texp_{x,x+5}^{t,t+1}} \tag{3}$$

$$GER_i^x = 5*\sum_{i=1}^{10} SERi_{x,x+5}^{t,t+1} \tag{4}$$

where:

$Entrepreneurship_{x,x+5}^{t,t+1}$ is the number of undertakings in the age group x, $x + 5$ and the period t, $t + 1$. These cases concern those who were undertaking a business as self-employment or for an employer and claimed to be carrying out an action such as obtaining a commercial register, elaboration of an action plan, etc. to start up the business (variable SUACTS of the APS database).

$Texp_{x,x+5}^{t,t+1}$ is the exposure time of the entrepreneurs until they experience the event of creating the enterprise. As the dates of these events are not available in the data source, the denominator is made up of the number of adults interviewed in each five-year group which at a certain time take the risk of setting up an enterprise.

$SER_{x,x+5}^{t,t+1}$ is the ratio between the number of declared entrepreneurships and the population in the age group x, $x + 5$ interviewed by the APS, which is called the Specific Entrepreneurship Rate of the age group x, $x + 5$ of the period t, $t + 1$.

GER_i^x. The Global Entrepreneurship Rate in the period i is the sum of the $SER_{x,x+5}^{t,t+1}$ in the ten five-year groups between the ages of 18 and 64 multiplied by 5 (convention of demography that represent the five-year groups).

GER is a real number that represents the number of entrepreneurships per adult at the end of their productive life, under the assumption of constant risk to undertake an enterprise. SER are also small real numbers, so for their interpretation they are multiplied by 1,000 to express the number of undertakings per 1,000 adults in the age group x, $x + 5$.

2.8 Results: Estimation of the Specific Entrepreneurship Rate

Using the information available in the Adult Population Survey (APS) of GEM Colombia, the SER are estimated by five-year age groups and the GER for the 2008 through 2017 series.

Figure 2.4 shows patterns that differ from others. In 2010 the Specific Entrepreneurship Rates are the lowest of the ten years observed with a significant gap related to the series. The group aged 18–19 presents the highest SER of all age groups, which means that they are the most entrepreneurial, except for 2008. After the first group a drop can be appreciated in the 20–24 age group in all the years. In later ages an oscillatory movement is observed that decreases towards the older ages, which is consistent, since the motivation to undertake a new enterprise is expected to decrease with age.

The 18–19 age group reaches the highest level of all groups in 2017 with 95.6 undertakings per 1,000 adults (see Table 2.2). This group experienced growth during the periods 2010–2013 and 2014–2017, although there were two minimum points in 2010 with 33.52 and in 2014 with 55.78 undertakings per 1,000.

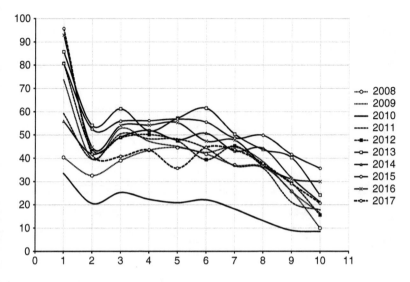

Figure 2.4 Specific Entrepreneurship Rates by Five-year Age Groups Expressed in Rates per 1,000 Adults Interviewed.

Source: Own calculations using the APS database 2008–2017 for Colombia.

Notes:

Axis X: age groups.

Axis Y: SER by group.

Table 2.2 Specific Entrepreneurship Rates per 1,000 Adults

Age Group	2008	2009	2010	2011	2012	2013	2014	2015	2016	2017
18–19	40.32	73.58	33.52	59.19	80.68	85.65	55.78	80.58	92.86	95.65
20–24	32.56	39.72	20.54	39.56	43.7	54.02	41.78	52.47	44.75	41.76
25–29	38.96	52.78	25.23	50.47	48.85	61.21	49.04	55.84	53.99	40.74
30–34	43.4	47.21	22.31	48.26	50.11	51.67	51.87	56.05	54.15	43.56
35–39	44.53	45.01	20.86	48.24	47.42	57.14	47.78	56.81	55.2	35.66
40–44	41.78	42.46	22.1	44.23	39.36	61.46	50.65	55.44	47.31	44.66
45–49	37.04	44.77	18.14	36.71	45.24	50.3	43.01	48.62	47.73	43.6
50–54	36.36	38.53	13.13	35.7	36.64	43.66	44.16	49.75	37.04	37.76
55–59	25.71	25.69	8.95	21.01	29.28	40.17	31.54	41.54	31.03	29.05
60–64	9.92	16.43	8.46	17.74	15.52	24.07	21.05	35.57	29.92	20.61

Source: Own calculations using the APS database 2008–2017 for Colombia.

You will observe in Figure 2.5 that the age groups 20–24, 25–29, 35–39 and 40–44 show a similar pattern in terms of the declines and increases in the rates over the decade. The lowest point is observed in 2010 with 20.54 undertakings per 1,000 in the 20–24 group, 25.23 in the 25–29 group, and 20.86 in the 35–39 group. In addition, the highest

Figure 2.5 Specific Entrepreneurship Rates for Each Five-year Age Group.
Source: Own calculations using the APS database 2008–2017 for Colombia.

levels over the decade fluctuate between 50 and 60 undertakings per 1,000 in these age groups.

Group 30–34 reflects greater stability in the SER curve. Although the 2010 mark is observed with the lowest entrepreneurship rates at the time of observation (22.31) for the other years the SER has an average value of 50 entrepreneurships per 1,000 adults.

Group 45–49 resembles group 30–34 excepting a slight drop in 2014. The level of entrepreneurship fluctuates between 40 and 50 per 1,000, and as a drop is noted as we move forward in the age group.

Groups 50–54 and 55–59 reflect a decrease in the level of entrepreneurship at these ages. The peak of 2010 is lower than in the previous ages (approximately ten undertakings per 1,000) and the behavior pattern for the rest of the years is unstable: between 30 and 50 entrepreneurships per 1,000.

Finally, the older adult 60–64 group shows a different curve than the others. It reveals an increasing oscillating behavior over the decade. Its lowest peak is not in 2010; rather, a maximum is prominent in 2015, with 35.57 entrepreneurships per 1,000. This could indicate a greater propensity for older adults to undertake an enterprise in accordance with their exit from the formal labor market, as other studies have found (Maritz et al., 2015).

The rates allow us to characterize entrepreneurship in the adult population aged 18–64 interviewed by the GEM in five-year age groups, a tool previously unavailable. This heterogeneity of entrepreneurship enables us to evidence the variability of the dynamics of entrepreneurship according to age, important information for decision making in public policy.

2.9 Results: The Global Entrepreneurship Rate

The GER can be estimated from the SER which is the summary indicator of entrepreneurship for the year t. Figure 2.6 shows the behavior of GER from 2008–2017. Taking 2008 as an example, the GER indicates that an average 1.753 entrepreneurships per adult aged 18 and 64 are estimated under the assumption of a constant propensity to undertake.

As expected, being a summary indicator, GER is a reflection of the behavior of the SER by five-year age groups. A minimum point is observed in 2010 with a GER of 0.966; subsequently the behavior shows fluctuations in an interval of 2.006 and 2.663 entrepreneurships per adult in Colombia. It should be noted that the GER has been increasing intermittently to approach an average of three entrepreneurships per

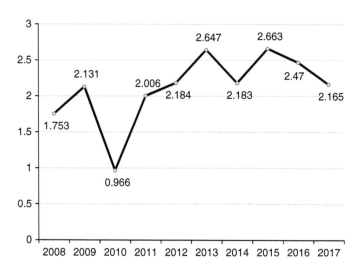

Figure 2.6 Colombian Global Entrepreneurship Rate, 2008–2017.
Source: Own calculations using the APS database 2008–2017 for Colombia GEM.

adult in 2013 and 2015. However, over the past three years this rate has decreased close to two entrepreneurships per adult.

2.10 Conclusions

The measurement of entrepreneurship through the concept of rate allows us to approach the phenomenon empirically through data. The rate is a measure that allows us to assess the risk of exposure to an event and is a proxy to the probability of occurrence of the phenomenon under study, which is very useful information for the generation of mathematical models. In that sense the GER is a rate that measures the risk to undertake an enterprise under conditions of data available, namely APS of GEM (Stewart, 2007: 270; Parra & Argote, 2017, 2018). In addition, the theoretical concept of rate eliminates the bias of size of the sample that, as we explained above, demonstrates high variability.

It is feasible to estimate the SER and GER based on APS GEM data and the results obtained allow for evaluation of the entrepreneurship dynamics of the population sample by five-year age groups. These indicators inform us of the levels of entrepreneurship in a given population. In addition, the method is replicable and rigorous, and has the strength of being comparable between different populations, since the GER can be calculated for the different countries that make up GEM, in support of decision making in public policy on entrepreneurship.

Based on the article by Henrekson and Sanandaji (2014), in which they measure Schumpeterian entrepreneurship through the rate of billionaire entrepreneurs, the changes in the SER and GER curves may be attributed to changes in self-employment levels. That is, as the economy improves and unemployment decreases, the level of entrepreneurship in Colombia decreases which turns out to be a positive aspect for the country's economy. On the other hand, if entrepreneurship increases we could interpret it as a negative indicator of the economy as several studies indicate, more recent entrepreneurships are associated with self-employment or micro-enterprises of fewer than ten employees, who develop their activities in the service sector and in subsistence economies rather than in Schumpeterian enterprises (Henrekson & Sanandaji, 2014; Parra, Argote & Farro, 2018; Astebro & Robinson, 2016; Audretsch et al., 2016; Kantis et al., 2012).

Compared to other measures of entrepreneurship, the proposed methodology for the construction of specific and global rates presents a way of approaching the measurement of risk to entrepreneurship based on the theoretical mathematical concepts of demography and statistics. Although the theoretical rate was not calculated as such due to the lack of data on dates, this does not imply that in the moment of having data of dates the Argote algorithm (2017) can be applied and thus improve the accuracy of the estimates.

References

Acs, Z. J. & Szerb, L. (2007). Entrepreneurship, economic growth and public policy. *Small Business Economics*, 28(2–3), 109–122.

Acs, Z. & Szerb, L. (2009). The Global Entrepreneurship Index (GEINDEX). *Foundations and Trends® in Entrepreneurship*, 5(5), 341–435. http://dx.doi.org/10.1561/0300000027.

Acs, Z. J., Autio, E. & Szerb, L. (2014). National systems of entrepreneurship: Measurement issues and policy implications. *Research Policy*, 43(3), 476–494.

Acs, Z., Desai, S. & Klapper, F. (2007). A comparison of GEM and the World Bank Group entrepreneurship data. In *Third GEM Research Conference: Entrepreneurship, Economic Development and Public Policy*.

Acs, Z., Szerb, L. & Lloyd, A. (2018). The global entrepreneurship index. In A. Lloyd (Ed.), *Global Entrepreneurship Index 2018*. The Global Entrepreneurship and Development Institute, Washington, DC, pp. 1–44.

Akerlof, G. & Shiller, J. R. (2016). La economía de la manipulación, como caemos como incautos en las trampas del mercado. *Deusto S.A. Ediciones*, Grupo Planeta, Madrid.

Argote Cusi, M. (2003). Evaluación de la calidad del dato. In Estimación de la distribución estadística de la Tasa Global de Fecundidad mediante remuestreo, descargado: http://conocimientoabierto.flacso.edu.mx/tesis/103.

Argote Cusi, M. (2007). Estimación de la distribución estadística de la Tasa Global de Fecundidad. *Papeles de Población*, 54(13), 87–113.

Argote Cusi, M. (2009). Comparación y evaluación de la distribución estadística del estimador de la tasa global de fecundidad de Bolivia en 1998 y 2003. *Papeles de Población*, 62(15), 201–222.

Argote Cusi, M. (2015). Sensitivity analysis of projections population. *Papeles de Población*, 84(21), 45–67.

Argote Cusi, M. & Parra, L. (2018). Working Paper: Evaluación de la Calidad del Dato GEM. Training Seminar using GEM data for Scientific Publications, developed 4–8 June 2018, Bogotá, Colombia. https://universidadean.edu.co/es/noticias/fuimos-sede-de-importante-seminario-de-datos-del-gem.

Astebro, Z. A. T. & Robinson, D. A. (2016). Public policy to promote entrepreneurship: A call to arms. *Small Business Economics*, 47, 35–51.

Audretsch, D. B., Kuratko, D. F. & Link, A. N. (2016). Dynamic entrepreneurship and technology-based innovation. *Journal of Evolutionary Economics*, 26(3), 603–620.

Cantillon, R. (2015 [1755]). *An Essay on the Nature of Trade in General.* The Liberty Fund, Indianapolis, IN.

Chowdhury, F., Terjesen, S. & Audretsch, D. (2015). Varieties of entrepreneurship: Institutional drivers across entrepreneurial activity and country. *European Journal of Law and Economics*, 40(1), 121–148.

Entrepreneurship Research Conference (2017). Babson College Entrepreneurship Research Conference (BCERC) and Doctoral Consortium co-sponsored by The University of Oklahoma, USA, June 7–10.

GEM (2017). Global Report 2017. www.gemconsortium.org/report/49812.

GEM (2018). Training seminar for scientific publications using GEM data. https://universidadean.edu.co/es/noticias/fuimos-sede-de-importante-seminario-de-datos-del-gem.

Gómez, L., López, S., Hernández, N., Galvis, M., Varela, R., Moreno, J., Pereira, F., Parra, L., Matíz, F., Cediel, G. & Martínez, P. (2018). *GEM Colombia: Estudio de la Actividad Empresarial en 2017.* UNINORTE, Barranquilla.

Gut Allan (2013). *Probability: A Graduate Course* (Vol. 75). Springer Science & Business Media, New York.

Henrekson, M. & Sanandaji, T. (2014). Small business activity does not measure entrepreneurship. *Proceedings of the National Academy of Sciences*, 111(5), 1760–1765.

Kantis, H., Federico, J. & Menéndez, C. (2012). Políticas de fomento al emprendimiento dinámico en América Latina: tendencias y desafíos. CAF Working Paper No. 2012/09, August 2012.

Maritz, A., Zolin, R., De Waal, A., Fisher, R., Perenyi, A. & Eager, B. (2015). Senior entrepreneurship in Australia: Active ageing and extending working lives. *International Journal of Organizational Innovation*, 7(1), 1–39.

Moreno-Altamirano, A., López-Moreno, S. & Corcho-Berdugo, A. (2000). Principales medidas en epidemiología. *Salud pública de México*, 42, 337–348.

Parra, L. & Argote, M. (2013). La gestión en el proceso de creación empresarial: el caso de IN3 de la Universidad EAN de Colombia. Emprendimiento: diferentes aproximaciones. Universidad EAN: Bogotá.

Parra, L. & Argote, M. (2017). Data analytics to characterize university-based companies for decision making in business development programs. In E. Rodriguez, *Data Analytics Applications in Latin America and Emerging Economies*, pp. 187–205. CRC Press, Abingdon, pp. 187–205.

Parra, L. & Argote, M. (2018). *Academia, emprendimiento e investigación empresarial: homenaje a la Universidad EAN en sus 50 años*. Ediciones Universidad EAN, Bogotá.

Parra, L., Argote, M. & Farro, T. (2018). Emprendimiento Universitario: Análisis de contraste entre la Universidad EAN – Colombia y la Universidad Continental – Perú. In L. Parra & M. Argote, *Academia, emprendimiento e investigación empresarial: homenaje a la Universidad EAN en sus 50 años*. Ediciones Universidad EAN, Bogotá.

Pressat, Roland (2000). *El análisis demográfico: Métodos, resultados, aplicaciones*. Fondo de cultura Económica, Mexico City.

Preston, S. H., Heuveline, P. & Guillot, M. (2001). *Demography: Measuring and Modelling Population Processes*. Blackwell, Oxford.

Reynolds, P., Bosma, N., Autio, E., Hunt, S., De Bono, N., Servais, I. & Chin, N. (2005). Global entrepreneurship monitor: Data collection design and implementation 1998–2003. *Small Business Economics*, 24(3), 205–231.

Rowland, D. T. (2003). *Demographic Methods and Concepts*. Oxford University Press, New York.

Schumpeter, J. A. (1980 [1934]). Change and the Entrepreneur. In *The Theory of Economic Development*. Oxford University Press, Oxford.

Siegel, J. S. & Swanson, D. A. (2004). *The Methods and Materials of Demography* (2nd edn). Elsevier, San Diego, CA.

Stewart, I. (2007). *La historia de las matemáticas, en los últimos 10.000 años*. Editorial Crítica, Barcelona.

Urbano, D., Aparicio, S. & Audretsch, D. (2018). Twenty-five years of research on institutions, entrepreneurship, and economic growth: What has been learned? *Small Business Economics*, 53(1), 21–49.

3 Forecast Entrepreneurship Population with Fuzzy Time Series

If we cannot avoid error we should recognize its existence.

(Argote, 2018)

A book about methodology for the calculation of metrics of a social phenomenon such as entrepreneurship could not be exempt from a chapter on forecasting. Prediction methods are the tip of the iceberg within what is called "sophisticated methods" in applied mathematics and statistics and the forecasting is a subdiscipline of prediction in which we are making predictions about the future on the basis of time-series data. In addition, as part of the latest technologies for smart data management (analytics) to support decision making, prediction is the process that represents the highest level of knowledge in organizations, as mentioned by Kopsco and Pachamanova (2017: 2) in their article "Business value in predictive and prescriptive Analytics models" (see also Argote & Parra, 2017).

Prediction is approached from various disciplines in order to predict the behavior of data to anticipate the future, which is very important in resource planning (financial, human, physical, etc.). In statistics the most common forecast models are those of linear regression re-presented by a line from which the parameters, to be projected at a later time, are obtained. Although this model is the simplest, it is the basis for understanding more complex methods that ultimately use the same mathematical principles. Therefore, it is not easy to know and understand linear regression, as well as its application.

Another discipline that broadens the vision of social system mod-eling is demography. Although it is not well known and developed in Latin American countries, demography is a discipline that makes use of actuarial methods, for the measurement and calculation of demo-graphic phenomena, using population data. In this way, demography provides a mathematical apparatus for population forecasts when considering fertility, mortality and migration rates, which are the basic parameters that define a population.

According to the above, there is a need for modeling the behavior of the entrepreneurial population and to forecast it because there are no references in the literature. In a global context of economic deceleration with an increasingly less protectionist state and high rates of unemployment, the subject of entrepreneurship has become important and has been included on the agenda of many countries as an alternative to the economic development of nations. From the data point of view, the *Global Entrepreneurship Monitor* (GEM) was born in 1999 with the interest of collecting information on worldwide entrepreneurship that supports decision making in public policy. It is this source of data that allows for the monitoring of entrepreneurship behavior at country and world levels through *Total Early Entrepreneurship Activity* (TEA), whose concept and methodology are reviewed in detail in Chapters 1 and 2 (Bosma, Coduras, Litovsky & Seaman, 2012).

A detail that cannot be omitted is that the basis of forecasting is the quality and validity of data. There is a rule in the modeling area that says, *"Garbage in, garbage out"*. This means that if there is no quality data, regardless of the model, it will give us erroneous or useless results for decision making. Therefore, an evaluation of data quality (EDQ) is essential, and for this reason the book dedicates Chapter 4 to presenting an EDQ methodology that readers cannot find elsewhere in the literature. This is why having a rich source of data on entrepreneurship such as the one provided by GEM, and after an Evaluation of Data Quality (see Chapter 1), it becomes feasible to apply the *Fuzzy Time Series* (FTS) method to forecast the entrepreneurship population.

It should be noted that the previous experience in the FTS modeling by authors (see e.g., Argote, 2018; Song & Chissom, 1993; Abbasov & Mamedova, 2003; Vovan, 2019; Mohammand & Hamisu, 2017; Burdey, Ali & Khan, 2018; Aladag, Aladag, Mentes & Egrioglu, 2012; Bas et al., 2014) constitute a robust theoretical basis for the application of this methodology in other areas. In Latin America in 2012, Argote started applying FTS to forecast the Mexican population, since Mexico is a country rich in population data and with a historical tradition of collecting information and population forecasting using traditional methods. This wealth of information on prediction in Mexico allows Argote to compare its results with other estimates made by official institutions, as well as other researchers, to conclude that the FTS method is coherent, requires little data and presents results with fewer errors than the others (Argote, 2018).

Thus, considering the access to data on entrepreneurship in Colombia that the GEM has collected annually since 2008 and with the previous experience of applying the FTS method to model data of the Mexican population, the challenge "forecast the entrepreneurial population" was born, and whose methodology and results are represented in this chapter. Because GEM Colombia applies the Adult Population Survey (APS) to a sample of the total population, the size of which may vary depending on the budget, it has been convenient not to take into account the absolute data of the population but to build a rate[1] which eliminates the bias of the sample size in order to capture as faithfully as possible the variations in the entrepreneurial population. This chapter details the "methodology for calculating The Global Entrepreneurship Rate". In this particular theoretical-mathematical scenario, it is relevant to take the present case as an example within the research line "metrics on entrepreneurship" as an embryonic development.

This chapter provides theoretical and methodological contributions, on the one hand in innovative entrepreneurship metrics, and on the other hand in the adaptation of the FTS method to samples of the total population.

3.1 Forecasting Methods

Nicolas Nassim Taleb (2007) believes that prediction as part of the science of uncertainty is an almost impossible task, since the probability of predicting unexpected events is very low, almost nil. However, the history of mathematics shows us that the modeling of social phenomena through mathematical functions, which include variables that explain the behavior, has favored the theoretical and empirical development of science (Zhi-xin, Hong-bin & An-min, 2009).

In this sense, this section presents forecast methods from the perspective of awareness of error, deepening in the handling of uncertainty which makes the models more robust in search of better estimates. It is not feasible to accurately predict the future, but it is feasible to generate a set of scenarios that allow us to control error. Without a doubt, this is a very useful tool for decision makers who need data and arguments on which to base the formulation of strategic actions (Sullivan & Woodall, 1994).

3.1.1 Traditional Methods

Although there is extensive literature on forecasting methods, this section considers as traditional methods those that come from demography as actuarial science. In demography, it is very important to forecast population and its distribution at disaggregated levels, with the objective of planning resources and services. The most used method is the one that considers the following general equation (Argote, 2015, 2018):

$$P_{t+1} = P_t + N_t - D_t + I_t - E_t \tag{1}$$

where N_t are the births in t, D_t the deaths, I_t the immigration and E_t the emigration, which balance the "compensating equation" to determine the population in t + 1. The four components are represented by their annual frequency rates (specific fertility rates, mortality rate and net migration rate) which are forecast under different behavioral hypotheses. This method is used in demography in a standard way and adapts to different social contexts, especially in those where the availability and quality of information is poor (CEPAL, 2009: 29–33; Argote, 2015).

The traditional methods are subject to various demographic assumptions such as constancy and equilibrium that are not intrinsic to nonlinear behaviors (Keyfitz, 1981; Rayer, 2008).[2] The strength of the method by components is its simplicity and its logic resembles a hydraulic system in which the total population can be assumed to be the amount of water in a tank filled with births and migrant populations, and is emptied with emigrations and deaths, and to have a certain estimated population level which is forecast over time under behavior assumptions of the rates that regulate these levels (Argote, 2015).

3.1.2 Non-traditional Methods

For the purposes of this chapter non-traditional forecast methods are those that fit within the stochastic or probabilistic methods (Zhi-xin et al., 2009). The change from actuarial to stochastic methods implies a conceptual transformation of how demography is conceived to open up new paradigms (Alho, 2014; Alho & Spencer, 1985). Since 1909 population projection exercises have been carried out using stochastic methods such as those of Lee (1998), Lee and Tuljapurkar (2000) and, in 2006, Alho and Spencer, who quantify the demographic uncertainty through the forecasting population of 18 European countries. In Latin America Ordorica (1995) applies the Kalman filter to estimate the Mexican population at a national level. Among other related works are those of Kesseli and Galindo, González and Guerrero, Garcia Guerrero and Ordorica, and Garcia Guerrero, discussed and analyzed by Argote (2018), who proposes a new projection method applying fuzzy time series, the results of which show greater precision than the previous ones in the case of Mexico.

Another non-traditional forecasting population line is the one that uses the resampling technique (bootstrap) to obtain the statistical distribution of a rate. In 2015 Argote, with available information about Bolivia, estimated the statistical distribution by a sampling of the population up until 2003 and projected to 2006. The innovation of Argote (2012) is that although it applies the traditional methods "by components" to forecast population, it takes as an input to the model a stochastic parameter: the distribution by sampling of the Global Fertility Rates, which transform the original model, to result in a statistic distribution by a sampling of the population forecast (Argote, 2007, 2009, 2012, 2015, 2016).

Unlike the previous ones, this chapter focuses on the methodology and application of fuzzy logic to the projection of data series, and as a result deepens in the fuzzy time series (FTS). The theory of *Fuzzy Sets* comes from the area of artificial intelligence, with the aim of modeling the approximate knowledge through heuristic methods which are at present heavily used in the face of the development of computing capacities (Silverman et al., 2013). The logic behind artificial intelligence models is to create models similar to human reasoning. This is a different logic from the traditional methods, so it is important to review definitions and concepts (Egrioglu, Bas, Aladag & Yolcu, 2016).

3.2 Fuzzy Time Series

The complexity of reasoning can be constructed from simple concepts such as elements, sets, their relationships and their generalization when considering infinite sets. It is in this way that the fuzzy set theory takes up the concept of sets and develops the construction of theorems to model approximations (Zhi-xin et al., 2009).

> The mathematics of fuzzy sets works with sets that have no perfectly defined limits, that is, the transition between membership and non-membership of a variable to a set is gradual. These sets are characterized by membership functions, which give flexibility to modeling using linguistic expressions, such as tall, medium, low etc., that is, work in greyscale in contrast with dichotomous states such as black and white.
>
> (Argote, 2016: 6)

3.2.1 General Characteristics of Fuzzy Sets

A *fuzzy set* expresses the degree of belonging to the set of each element; the fuzzy set A and X can be defined as the set of organized pairs:

$$A = \{((x, \mu_A(x))|x \in X\} \qquad (2)$$

where $\mu_A(x)$ is the membership function to the set.

The *membership function* assigns for each element of X a degree membership to set A. The value of this function is in the range between 0 and 1 being the value for maximum membership. If the value of this function were restricted to 0 and 1, there would be a classic or non-fuzzy set. This function is not unique. The most frequently used functions are trapezoidal, singleton, triangular (T), type S, exponential and type II (bell shaped). Due to space restrictions of this chapter, the details of the mathematical characteristics of fuzzy sets can be found in Zadeh (1965, 1973), Rutkowska (2002), Jang, Sun & Mizutani (1997), Nauck & Kruse (1997), Kosko (1992), Martín del Brio & Sanz (2002), Martín, Medrano, Pollán & Sanz (1970), and Dubois, Ostasiewicz & Prade (2000).

3.2.2 Definitions and Theorems

Definition 1. Being $Y(t) \in R^1$ where $t = 0, 1, 2, \ldots$ a time series. If $f_i(t)$ is a fuzzy set in $Y(t)$ y $F(t) = \{f_1(t), F_2(t), \ldots\}$ then F (t) is a fuzzy time series in Y(t).

Definition 2. It is assumed that $F(t)$ is an event caused by $F(t-1)$ only; that is, $F(t-1) \rightarrow F(t)$ the intervening relationship is expressed as:

$$F(t) = F(t-1)° R(t, t-1) \qquad (3)$$

where $R(t, t-1)$ is a diffuse relationship and is called the first-order model of $F(t)$.

Definition 3. Assume that $R(t, t-1)$ is a first-order model of $F(t)$. If for each t, $R(t, t-1)$ is independent of t, then for all t, $R(t, t-1) = R(t-1, t-2)$ $F(t)$ is called a fuzzy time series invariant in time.

Considering the previous definitions, two important theorems are presented:

Theorem 1. Being $F(t)$ a fuzzy time series. If for t, $F(t) = F(t-1)$ then $F(t)$ is a fuzzy time series invariant in time.

Theorem 2. If $F(t)$ is a fuzzy time series, $F(t) = F(t-1)$ for all t; and $F(t)$ has finite elements $f_i(t)$ then:

$$R(t, t-1) = f_{i1}(t-1) \times f_{j1}(t) \cup f_{i2}(t-2)$$
$$\times f_{j2}(t-1) \cup ... \cup f_{im}(t-m) \times f_{jm}(t-m+1) \tag{4}$$

where $m > 0$.

This theorem implies that, in the case of a fuzzy time series, it is very simple and convenient to work with a first-order model. Since infinite fuzzy sets can be rigorously defined in any universe, before any successive point t_1 and t_2, the same fuzzy set is maintained, and from this we can obtain a fuzzy time series invariable in time (Song & Chissom, 1993).

3.3 The Use of Fuzzy Time Series to Forecast Data

The first to make the mathematical formulation of the fuzzy time series were Song and Chissom in 1993, using the theoretical development of fuzzy sets made by Zadeh in 1965. Since that time, several authors have explored these techniques and made more precise estimates. The advances in this line of research have been made in two areas in the improvement of the methodology for increasing the accuracy of the results and in the application to other fields. In the first field Song and Chissom improve their models, including time series, time variations and neural networks (1993, 1994), and Chen and Hsu (2004) propose a new interval division methodology that improves the estimation of the projection of student enrollment at the University of Alabama in the US (Chen, 2002).

In the second field there is a record of the application of fuzzy time series for temperature prediction (Chen & Hwang, 2000) and in demography. In 2003 Abbasov and Mamedova were able to use fuzzy time series for the projection of the Azerbaijan population based on historical data between 1980–2001. They used an invariant model over time and found the quality of the model to project the Azerbaijan population using sparse data (Argote, 2015). On the other hand, Sasu (2010) applied the methodology used by Abbasov and Mamedova (2003) for the Romanian population from 1988–2009 and found satisfactory results using fuzzy time series, which evidenced errors of less than 0.003 between the data observed and projected.

Recently, the most important development in this matter comes from Asia. Among others, Tai Vovan (2019), using the model of Abbasov and Mamedova (2003), put forward a new proposal, including in the FTS model algorithms for the estimation of two important parameters: the constant C (*Algorithm to find the appropriate value for the constant* C), and the number of intervals into which the universe of variations of the data series should be divided (*Algorithm to find the dividing intervals for the universal set*). They calibrate the model with cereal production data in India from 1966–2011 used by Ghosh, Chowdhury and Prajneshu (2015) and later applied the model to predict salt peaks in the Ca Mau province of southern Vietnam which is one of the areas most affected by climatic change. The results are compared with previous investigations with more optimal results in the minimization of error.

Burney, Ali and Khan (2018) incorporate into their proposal the "Huarng" method for the division of intervals of the universe of variations, a trapezoidal function for membership and propose a second-order model for the fuzzy data series. Yusuf, Mohammad and Hamisu (2017) apply an FTS for the projection of temperatures; unlike others, they propose a new way of finding the intervals of fuzzy sets through a mathematical model that improves the performance of FTS (see variations in Chen & Chen (2011), Chen & Tanuwijaya (2011), and Chen & Shiu (2007)).

3.4 Characteristics of the FTS-R Proposal

The importance of this chapter and this application is that the data series of a rate is used, which is a complex indicator whose calculation methodology is presented in Chapter 2 based on the data of the entrepreneurial population compiled by GEM Colombia. This chapter is the first attempt to verify the capabilities of the FTS model to forecast a rate with fuzzy time series, a model that will be called FTS-R from now on. Forecasting an indicator is chosen as the rate because this indicator eliminates the bias of the sample size that showed a significant increase between 2010–2012, which could affect the model (see Table 3.1).

The data series of the Global Entrepreneurship Rate (GER) are used from 2008–2017 (estimated in Chapter 2), which measure the average number of entrepreneurships set up by an adult aged 18–64 over the course of his or her productive life, under the assumption that the propensity to be an entrepreneur remains constant.[3] The GER is estimated from the Specific Entrepreneurship Rate (SER) as follows:

Table 3.1 GEM Colombia's Annual Distribution of the Total Entrepreneur and Active Entrepreneur Population, 2008–2017

Age Group	2008			2009			2010			2011			2012			2013			2014			2015			2016			2017		
	PT	PE	PEA	PT	PE	PEA	PT	PE	PEA	PT	PE	PEA	PT	PE	PEA	PT	PE	PEA	PT	PE	PEA	PT	PE	PEA	PT	PE	PEA	PT	PE	PEA
18–19	124	15	10	299	56	44	701	82	47	718	123	47	409	101	85	216	57	37	251	58	28	242	64	39	140	34	26	115	28	22
20–24	258	49	42	569	130	113	1,441	262	148	1,466	390	148	920	285	290	485	177	131	493	152	103	446	163	117	362	109	81	273	82	57
25–29	231	51	45	485	145	128	1,221	241	154	1,276	437	154	913	322	322	428	174	131	416	152	102	462	182	129	263	104	71	270	74	55
30–34	235	69	51	466	137	110	1,219	230	136	1,206	404	136	902	328	291	418	153	108	455	180	118	446	190	125	229	79	62	225	73	49
35–39	247	73	55	431	132	97	1,112	207	116	1,078	368	116	717	257	260	343	152	98	406	163	97	426	187	121	221	81	61	258	76	46
40–44	225	58	47	471	138	100	1,267	248	140	1,153	381	140	874	288	255	371	166	114	387	145	98	386	156	107	186	52	44	206	62	46
45–49	243	59	45	411	122	92	1,213	202	110	1,046	320	110	504	206	192	330	139	83	372	149	88	398	177	99	176	55	42	211	65	46
50–54	176	35	32	353	90	68	1,112	154	73	1,014	311	73	535	178	181	339	136	74	385	142	85	362	145	88	189	53	35	196	64	37
55–59	140	24	18	288	55	37	916	110	41	752	163	41	362	107	79	229	78	53	260	69	41	260	102	54	174	46	27	179	49	26
60–64	121	9	6	280	31	23	827	75	35	665	110	35	335	71	59	241	72	29	266	61	28	253	90	45	127	27	19	165	31	17
Total	2,000	442	351	4,053	1,036	812	11,029	1,801	1,000	10,374	3,007	1,000	6,471	2,143	2,014	3,400	1,304	851	3,691	1,271	780	3,681	1,456	924	2,067	640	468	2,098	604	401

Source: Own elaboration.

Notes:

PT: Adult population aged 18–64 interviewed by the APS Colombia.

PE: Population interviewed in the APS that respond whether they undertake an enterprise on their own account or for an employer.

PEA: Population interviewed in the APS that confirm whether they undertake an enterprise and also confirm that they are carrying out some action for entrepreneurship such as registration before the Chamber of Commerce, business plan, etc.

Table 3.2 GEM Colombia's Specific Rates of Entrepreneurship for 1,000 Adults Interviewed and Global Entrepreneurship Rate, 2008–2017

Age Group	2008	2009	2010	2011	2012	2013	2014	2015	2016	2017
18–19	40.32	73.58	33.52	59.19	80.68	85.65	55.78	80.58	92.86	95.65
20–24	32.56	39.72	20.54	39.56	43.7	54.02	41.78	52.47	44.75	41.76
25–29	38.96	52.78	25.23	50.47	48.85	61.21	49.04	55.84	53.99	40.74
30–34	43.4	47.21	22.31	48.26	50.11	51.67	51.87	56.05	54.15	43.56
35–39	44.53	45.01	20.86	48.24	47.42	57.14	47.78	56.81	55.2	35.66
40–44	41.78	42.46	22.1	44.23	39.36	61.46	50.65	55.44	47.31	44.66
45–49	37.04	44.77	18.14	36.71	45.24	50.3	43.01	48.62	47.73	43.6
50–54	36.36	38.53	13.13	35.7	36.64	43.66	44.16	49.75	37.04	37.76
55–59	25.71	25.69	8.95	21.01	29.28	40.17	31.54	41.54	31.03	29.05
60–64	9.92	16.43	8.46	17.74	15.52	24.07	21.05	35.57	29.92	20.61
TGE	**1.753**	**2.1309**	**0.9662**	**2.0056**	**2.184**	**2.6468**	**2.1833**	**2.6633**	**2.4699**	**2.1652**

Source: Own calculations based on the GEM Colombia data.

$$TEE_{x,x+5}^{t,t+1} = \frac{Entrepreneruships_{x,x+5}^{t,t+1}}{Texp_{x,x+5}^{t,t+1}} \tag{a}$$

$$TGE_i^x = 5 * \sum_{i=1}^{10} TEE_{x,x+5}^{t,t+1} \tag{b}$$

Table 3.2 presents the series of SER data from which the GER from 2008–2017 is estimated, which is the input data of the FTS-R model.

3.5 The Method

Being U in the discourse universe, $U = \{u_1, u_2, \ldots, u_n\}$ and A in the discourse universe, U is defined as follows:

$$= f_A(u_1)/u_1 + f_A(u_2)/u_2 + \ldots + f_A(u_n)/u_n \tag{5}$$

where f_A is a function of membership of A, $f_A:U \rightarrow [0, 1]$, $f_A(u_i)$ indicates the degree of membership of u_i in the fuzzy set A, $f_A(u_i) \in [0, 1]$ y $1 \leq i \leq n$.

Being $X(t)(t = \ldots, 0, 1, 2, \ldots)$ the discourse universe and subset of R, and being the fuzzy set $f_i(t)(i = 1, 2, \ldots)$ is defined in $X(t)$. Being $F(t)$ a collection of $f_i(t)(i = 1, 2, \ldots)$. Then $F(t)$ is called a fuzzy time series of $X(t)(t = \ldots 0, 1, 2, \ldots)$.

If $F(t)$ is caused by $F(t-1)$, that is, $F(t-1) \rightarrow F(t)$, then this relationship can be represented by $F(t) = F(t-1)°R(t, t-1)$, where the symbol "°" indicates the compound operator Max-Min; $R(t, t-1)$ is a fuzzy relationship between $F(t)$ y $F(t-1)$ and is called the first-order model of $F(t)$.

Being $F(t)$ a fuzzy time series and being $R(t, t-1)$ the first-order model of $F(t)$. If $R(t, t-1) = R(t-1, t-2)$ for any t, then $F(t)$ is called fuzzy time series invariant in time. If $R(t, t-1)$ is time dependent, that is, $R(t, t-1)$ can be different from $R(t-1, t-2)$ for any t, then $F(t)$ is called fuzzy time series variant in time.

Considering the above definitions, the forecasting method is carried out using the following steps:

Step 1: Define the discourse universe, the fuzzy sets and the linguistic variables.

Step 2: Partition the discourse universe in equal intervals.

Step 3: Determine the values of the linguistic variables represented by the variables into which the discourse universe was divided.

Step 4: Fuzzify the historical data (assign degrees of belonging in all cases):

$$\mu_{A^{mn}}(u_i) = \frac{1}{1 + [C * (U - u_m^i)]^2} \tag{6}$$

where A^{mn} is the fuzzy set that corresponds to the variation between the years (2008, 2017), C is a constant that in our case is 0.01, U is the discourse universe formed by the variations shown in Table 3.1 and u_m^i is the average point of the corresponding interval u_i. The fuzzy sets are defined in the universe U.

Step 5. Select the parameter w where $w > 1$, calculate the matriz R^w $(t, t - 1)$ and forecast the population as follows:

$$F(t) = F(t - 1) \circ R^w(t, t - 1) \tag{7}$$

where $F(t)$ is the forecast data of the population during the year t, $F(t - 1)$ is the fuzzyfied population of the year $t - 1$ and:

$$R^w(t, t - 1) = F^T(t - 2) \times F(t - 1) \cup F^T(t - 3)$$
$$\times F(t - 2) \cup \ldots \cup F^T(t - w) \times F(t - w + 1) \tag{8}$$

here w is called the "base model" that considers the number of years before time t, "$\times$" is the Cartesian product and T is the transposed operator.

Step 6. Fuzzifying the projected population. It is necessary to transform the answer so that it is not fuzzified; in this case the area centroid method is used (Jang, Sun & Mizutani, 1997):

$$V(t) = \frac{\sum_{i=1}^{5} \mu_t(u_i) \cdot u_m^i}{\sum_{i=1}^{5} \mu_t(u_i)} \tag{9}$$

where $\mu_t(u_i)$ is the calculated value of the membership function to the projected year t and u_m^i is the average value of the interval.

Step 7. The estimated error of the population projections according to the current methodology was calculated using the following formula:

$$\delta(t) = \frac{V^t_{obs} - V^t_{proy}}{N^t_{obs}} * 100$$

$$(10)$$

where V^t_{obs} is the variation of the population in the year t; V^t_{proy} is the variation of the projected population in the year t; and N^t_{obs} is the total observed population in the year t, $2008 \le t \le 2017$.

3.6 Results

The difference between the rates of the year t and the previous year gives us the variation between $[t-1, t]$. The "variation" column of Table 3.3 is represented in the discourse universe U. Allowing the minimum variation value of the Global Entrepreneurship Rate (GER) to be between $[t-1, t]$ = -1.16467 and the maximum value 1.03936, we have an interval in which the variations of the estimated GER fluctuate based on the GEM data over ten years (2008–2017). According to the methodology, $U = [V_{min} - D_1, V_{max} - D_2]$, where $D_1 = 0.1398$ and $D_2 = 0.11414$, in such a way that the discourse universe of the GER is $U = [-1.304536, 1.153457]$.

The discourse universe is divided into equal intervals. In the present case it is divided into five equal intervals that correspond to the linguistic variables defined in Table 3.3: u_1 = $[-1.304570; -0.812944]$, u_2 = $[-0.812944; -0.321318]$, $u_3 = [-0.321318; 0.170308]$, $u_4 = [0.170308; 0.661943]$, $u_5 = [0.661934; 1.153560]$. The midpoints of the intervals are presented for the estimation of the lowest average error $u^1_m = 1.058737$, $u^2_m = 0.567138$, $u^3_m = 0.075539$, $u^4_m = 0.416059$, $u^5_m = 0.907658$. The linguistic variable "Variation of the Global Entrepreneurship Rate" adopts the linguistic values shown in Table 3.3.

Table 3.4 shows fuzzy sets corresponding to each year. These sets are estimated based on the variation in the estimated GER according to the previous year and the membership function defined in equation (6) of the methodology.

Table 3.3 Linguistic Variables and Fuzzy Sets of the FTS-R Model

Linguistic Values	*Fuzzy Variables*
A1: Low Growth	LGER (-1.304570; -0.812944), A1
A2: Small Growth	SGER (-0.812944; -0.321318), A2
A3: Moderate Growth	MGER (-0.321318; 0.170308), A3
A4: Normal Growth	NGER (0.170308; 0.661943), A4
A5: High Growth	HGER (0.661934; 1.153560), A5

Source: Own elaboration.

Table 3.4 Data Series of the Global Entrepreneurship Rate, the Variation and the Membership Values, 2008–2017

Year	GER	Variation	Fuzzification of the Variations
2008	1.752953		
2009	2.130922	0.37797	$A^{09} = (0.99979363/u_1)$, $(0.99991069/u_2)$, $(0.99997943/u_3)$, $(0.99999985/u_4)$, $(0.99997194/u_5)$
2010	0.966244	-1.164678	$A^{10} = (0.99999888/u_1)$, $(0.9999643/u_2)$, $(0.99988139/u_3)$, $(0.99975019/u_4)$, $(0.99957073/u_5)$
2011	2.005605	1.039361	$A^{11} = (0.99955999/u_1)$, $(0.99974198/u_2)$, $(0.99987572/u_3)$, $(0.99996115/u_4)$, $(0.99999827/u_5)$
2012	2.183989	0.178385	$A^{12} = (0.99984698/u_1)$, $(0.99994442/u_2)$, $(0.99999355/u_3)$, $(0.99999435/u_4)$, $(0.99994682/u_5)$
2013	2.646793	0.462804	$A^{13} = (0.99976855/u_1)$, $(0.99989393/u_2)$, $(0.99997102/u_3)$, $(0.99999978/u_4)$, $(0.99998021/u_5)$
2014	2.183277	-0.463516	$A^{14} = (0.99996457/u_1)$, $(0.99999893/u_2)$, $(0.99998495/u_3)$, $(0.99992264/u_4)$, $(0.99981202/u_5)$
2015	2.663349	0.480072	$A^{15} = (0.99976326/u_1)$, $(0.99989035/u_2)$, $(0.99996913/u_3)$, $(0.99999959/u_4)$, $(0.99998172/u_5)$
2016	2.469924	-0.193425	$A^{16} = (0.99992513/u_1)$, $(0.99998603/u_2)$, $(0.99999861/u_3)$, $(0.99996285/u_4)$, $(0.99987878/u_5)$
2017	2.165196	-0.304729	$A^{17} = (0.99994315/u_1)$, $(0.99999311/u_2)$, $(0.99999475/u_3)$, $(0.99994805/u_4)$, $(0.99985303/u_5)$

Source: Own elaboration.

Table 3.5 Results of the GER Projection, Retrospective Stage, 2013–2017

Year	Observed		Forecast		Error	Average
	GER	Variation	GER	Variation		
2013	2.64679	0.4628	2.57131	NA	NA	0.06421
2014	2.18328	-0.46352	2.1077	-0.31245	-0.06919	
2015	2.66335	0.48007	2.58786	0.32901	0.05672	
2016	2.46992	-0.19342	2.39437	-0.04239	-0.06115	
2017	2.1652	-0.30473	2.08963	-0.45584	0.06979	

Source: Own calculations.

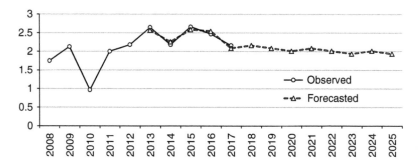

Figure 3.1 Forecast of Global Entrepreneurship Rate, 2017–2025.
Source: Own elaboration using the GEM Columbia data.

Once the matrix of fuzzified values is obtained, step 5 of equations (7) and (8) is applied to obtain as a result the matrix $F(t)$ of $1 \times n$. The matrix is defuzzified through equation (9) to obtain the projected value. Table 3.5 shows the projected values in retrospective stages, that is, estimates for the series of data from the past to the present. By applying the formula (10) an average error of 0,06421 allows the evaluation of the adjustment of the FTS-R model.

According to Figure 3.1, the projected curve is adjusted to the data observed between 2013–2017. The data projection starts during the period from 2017–2025, in which the methodology is applied considering the matrix of fuzzified values of the variations $R^w(t)$ or the first-order model, to give the results of the prospective stage shown in the "Forecasted 2019" column of Table 3.6.

Table 3.6 shows that the results of the GER estimates with the fuzzy time series are consistent.

Table 3.6 GER Forecasted, Retrospective and Prospective Stages, 2008–2025

Stage	Year	Observed: Data Estimated by Argote & Parra (2017)	Forecasted 2019 FTS-R
Retrospective Stage	2008	1.75295	NA
	2009	2.13092	NA
	2010	0.96624	NA
	2011	2.0056	NA
	2012	2.18399	NA
	2013	2.64679	2.57131
	2014	2.18328	2.25885
	2015	2.66335	2.58786
	2016	2.46992	2.54548
	2017	2.1652	2.08963
Prospective Stage	2018	NA	2.16513
	2019	NA	2.08949
	2020	NA	2.01405
	2021	NA	2.08957
	2022	NA	2.01408
	2023	NA	1.9385
	2024	NA	2.01399
	2025	NA	1.93844

Source: Own elaboration.
Note: NA: Not applicable.

3.7 Conclusions

This method has proven to be robust and allows modeling of the nonlinear behavior of the Global Entrepreneurship Rate, which is a summary indicator of entrepreneurship. The average error between the observed and forecasted data of the GER is 0.06421. When comparing the historical data curve of the GER with the estimated curve with FTS-R, it can be observed that the historical trend of the data is adjusted and maintained.

In the case of samples of the total population, for example, the entrepreneurial population of GEM Colombia, it is pertinent to use a series of input data to the FTS-R model a rate or proportion that eliminates the bias of the sample size. Consequently, the work of Argote (detailed in Chapter 2) made it possible to use the data series of the GER and SER to carry out the research whose results are included in this chapter.

In the future, it could be interesting to apply the methodology to forecast the SER by five-year age groups, which allows for the evaluation of the heterogeneous behavior of entrepreneurship by age, an aspect not made visible by a summary indicator such as GER. This will enable accessing information at more disaggregated levels which is useful for decision makers from different government levels.

Finally, the methods originating from Artificial Intelligence that incorporate the concepts of probability, optimization, computation and precision offer a new perspective on forecasting population that is interesting to consider in support of public policy decisions, in this case entrepreneurship.

3.8 Triggering Questions

Considering the methodology presented here for the application of fuzzy time series (FTS) in different areas:

Modeling with fuzzy time series, how well does it fit with the real behavior of social systems?

Based on the previous case, is the methodology feasible in applying a series of rates to eliminate the bias of population samples?

Based on the above methodology, how can SERs be estimated?

What can we infer from the results of the FTS-R model?

Notes

1 Theoretical definition of rate: the number of people exposed to experiencing the event between the exposure time measured in person years. Because the theoretical definition requires a longitudinal data design, it is neither easy nor feasible to calculate it frequently (Argote, 2007). However, under certain demographic assumptions, the law of large numbers and the central limit theorem, it can be assumed that the denominator approaches the average population over time during the period in which the rate is measured. Review the detail of the definition of a rate, specific dates and Global Entrepreneurship Rate in this chapter. This chapter uses the results of the calculation of this measure for 2008–2017 proposed and generated as a new entrepreneurship metric, presented in the *Training Seminar: Using GEM Data for Scientific Publications*. Bogotá, Colombia, June 2018, sponsored by the Global Entrepreneurship Monitor Consortium.

2 In the work of Argote (2007) there is a rigorous analysis on the subject of assumptions in demography and her thesis that methods that capture the nonlinear dynamics of populations are required.

3 The details of the estimation for the GER and the SER are found in Chapter 2. In this chapter only the results of the methodology developed in Chapter 2 are used.

References

Abbasov, A. & Mamedova, M. (2003). Application of fuzzy time series to population forecasting. *Vienna University of Technology*, 1, 545–552.

Aladag, S., Aladag, C. H., Mentes, T. & Egrioglu, E. (2012). A new seasonal fuzzy time series method based on the multiplicative neuron model and SARIMA. *Hacettepe Journal of Mathematics and Statistics*, 41(3), 145–163.

Alho, J. M. (2014). Forecasting demographic forecasts. *International Journal of Forecasting*, 30(4), 1128–1135.

Alho, J. M. & Spencer, B. D. (1985). Uncertain population forecasting. *Journal of the American Statistical Association*, 80(390), 306–314.

Alho, J. & Spencer, B. (2006). *Statistical Demography and Forecasting*. Springer Science & Business Media, New York.

Alho, J., Alders, M., Cruijsen, H., Keilman, N., Nikander, T. & Pham, D. Q. (2006). New forecast: Population decline postponed in Europe. *Statistical Journal of the United Nations Economic Commission for Europe*, 23(1), 1–10.

Argote Cusi, M. (2007). Estimation of the statistical distribution of the Global Fertility Rate. *Papeles de Población*, 54(13), 87–113.

Argote Cusi, M. (2009). Comparison and evaluation of the statistical distribution of the estimator of the total fertility rate of Bolivia in 1998 and 2003. *Papeles de Población*, 62(15), 201–222.

Argote Cusi, M. (2012). Analysis of sensitivity of births to small changes in the Global Fertility Rate. *Papeles de Población*, 72(18), 85–112.

Argote Cusi, M. (2015). Análisis de sensibilidad de proyecciones de población. *Papeles de Población*, 84, 45–67, April/June.

Argote Cusi, M. L. (2016). Uso de la lógica difusa en proyecciones de población. Paper presented in the XIII National Meeting of Demographic Research, 22–24 June, UNAM, Mexico.

Argote Cusi, M. L. (2018). El uso de lógica difusa en proyecciones de población: el caso de México. *Papeles de población*, 24(95), 273–301.

Argote Cusi, M. & Parra Bernal, L. D. (2017). Data analytics to characterize university-based companies for decision making in business development programs. In *Data Analytics Applications in Latin America and Emerging Economies*. CRC Press, Abingdon, pp. 187–205.

Bas, E., Uslu, V. R., Aladag, C., Yolcu, U. & Egrioglu, E. (2014). A modified genetic algorithm for forecasting fuzzy time series. *Applied Intelligence*, 41, 453–463.

Bosma, N., Coduras, A., Litovsky, Y. & Seaman, J. (2012). GEM Manual: A report on the design, data and quality control of the Global Entrepreneurship Monitor. *Global Entrepreneurship Monitor*, 9.

Burney, S. A., Ali, S. M. & Khan, M. S. (2018). A novel high order Fuzzy Time Series forecasting method with higher accuracy rate. *International Journal of Computer Science and Network Security*, 18(5), 13–40.

CEPAL (2009). Proyección de población. Demographic Observatory Latin American and Caribbean, Year IV, No. 7, April. Publication developed by Guiomar Bay.

Chen, S. M. (2002). Forecasting enrollments based on high-order fuzzy time series. *Cybernetics and Systems: An International Journal,* 33, 1–16.

Chen, S. M. & Chen, D. C. (2011). TAIEX forecasting based on fuzzy time series and fuzzy variation groups. *IEEE Transactions on Fuzzy Systems,* 19, 1–12.

Chen, S. M. & Hsu, C. C. (2004). A new method to forecast enrollments using fuzzy time series. *International Journal of Applied Science and Engineering,* 2(3), 234–244

Chen, S. M. & Hwang, J. R. (2000). Temperature prediction using fuzzy time series. *IEEE Transactions on Systems, Man, and Cybernetics-Part B: Cybernetics,* 30, 263–275.

Chen, S. M. & Kao, P. Y. (2013). TAIEX forecasting based on fuzzy time series, particle swarm optimization techniques and support vector machines. *Information Sciences,* 247, 62–71.

Chen, S. M. & Tanuwijaya, K. (2011). Fuzzy forecasting based on high-order fuzzy logical relationships and automatic clustering techniques. *Expert Systems with Applications,* 38, 15425–15437.

Chen, T. L. & Shiu, S. Y. (2007). A new clustering algorithm based on self-updating process. *In JSM Proceedings, Statistical Computing Section,* Salt Lake City, UT, pp. 2034–2038.

Dubois, D., Ostasiewicz, W. & Prade, H. (2000). Fuzzy sets: History and basic notions. In *Fundamentals of Fuzzy Sets.* Springer, Boston, MA, pp. 21–124.

Egrioglu, S., Bas, E., Aladag, C. H. & Yolcu, U. (2016). Probabilistic fuzzy time series method based on artificial neural network. *American Journal of Intelligent Systems,* 62(2), 42–47.

Ghosh, H., Chowdhury, S. & Prajneshu, S. (2015). An improved fuzzy time series method of forecasting based on L-R fuzzy. *Journal of Applied Statistics,* 43(6), 1128–1139.

Jang J. S. R., Sun, C-T. & Mizutani, E. (1997). *Neuro-Fuzzy and Soft Computing. A Computational Approach to Learning and Machine Intelligence.* Prentice-Hall, London.

Keyfitz, N. (1981). The limits of population forecasting. *Population and Development Review,* 27(4), 579–593. Ed. Population Council, Washington, DC.

Kopcso, D. & Pachamanova, D. (2017). Case article: Business value in integrating predictive and prescriptive analytics models. *INFORMS Transactions on Education.*

Kosko, B. (1992). *Neural Networks and Fuzzy Systems: A Dynamical Systems Approach to Machine Intelligence,* vol. 1. Prentice Hall, London.

Lee, R. D. & Tuljapurkar, S. (2000). Population forecasting for fiscal planning: Issues and innovations. Ed. UC Berkeley, CEDA. Available at https://escholarship.org/content/qt7n02r268/qt7n02r268.pdf.

Lee, S. M. (1998). Asian Americans: Diverse and growing. *Population Bulletin,* 53(2), 1.

Martín del Brío, B. & Sanz Molina, A. (2002). *Redes neuronales y sistemas difusos.* Alfaomega, Mexico City.

Martín, B., Medrano, N., Pollán, T. & Sanz, A. (1970). *Redes neuronales y sistemas borrosos: un libro de texto en español.* Ed. Universidad de Zaragoza.

Mohammad, A. & Hamisu, A. A. (2017). A novel two-factor high order fuzzy time series with applications to temperature and futures exchange forecasting. *Nigerian Journal of Technology*, 36(4), 1124–1134.

Nauck, D. & Kruse, R. (1997). A neuro-fuzzy method to learn fuzzy classification rules from data. *Fuzzy Sets and Systems*, 89, 277–288.

Rayer, S. (2008). Population forecast errors: A primer for planners. *Journal of Planning Education and Research*, 27(4), 417–430.

Rutkowska, D. (2002). Type 2 fuzzy neural networks: An interpretation based on fuzzy inference neural networks with fuzzy parameters. In *Fuzzy Systems*. Proceedings of the 2002 IEEE International Conferenc, vol. 2, pp. 1180–1185.

Sasu, A. (2010). An application of fuzzy time series to the Romanian population. *Bulletin of the Transilvania University of Brasov*, 3, 52.

Silverman, E., Bijak, J., Hilton, J., Cao, V. D. & Noble, J. (2013). When demography met social simulation: A tale of two modelling approaches. *Journal of Artificial Societies and Social Simulation*, 16(4), 9.

Song, Q. & Chissom, B. S. (1993). Fuzzy time series and its models. *Fuzzy Sets and Systems*, 54(3), 269–277.

Song, Q. & Chissom, B. S. (1994). Forecasting enrollments with fuzzy time series: Part II. *Fuzzy Sets and Systems*, 62(1), 1–8.

Sullivan, J. & Woodall, W. H. (1994). A comparison of fuzzy forecasting and Markov modeling. *Fuzzy Sets and Systems*, 64(3), 279–293.

Taleb, N. N. (2007). *El Cisne Negro, el impacto de la altamente improbable.* Editorial Paidós, Madrid.

Vovan, T. (2019). An improved fuzzy time series forecasting model using variations of data. *Fuzzy Optimization and Decision Making*, 18(2), 151–173.

Zadeh, L. A. (1965). Fuzzy sets. *Information and Control*, 8(3), 338–353.

Zadeh, L. A. (1973). Outline of a new approach to the analysis of complex systems and decision processes. *Systems, Man and Cybernetics, IEEE Transactions*, 1, 28–44.

Zhi-xin, J., Hong-bin, Z. & An-min, X. (2009). Research in method of complex system reliability evaluation based-on fuzzy sets. In *Intelligent Systems and Applications, 2009. ISA 2009. International Workshop*, pp. 1–4.

4 A Case Study of the Application of Big Data in Entrepreneurship

4.1 Introduction

Nowadays, access to several information systems is strategic support decision making. Under the premise that information is power, accessing the updated market information and population characterization studies is important, not only for any edge research but also for business intelligence (Martinez & Martinez, 2010; Cañibano & Sánchez, 2009).

While the United States and Europe have extensive literature on and experience of business and entrepreneurship (Rothaermel, Agung & Jiang, 2007), in Latin America the statistical information based on the characterization of the business network is at an embryonic stage, with some initiatives such as the Global Entrepreneurship Monitor (GEM) that gather information worldwide contemplating certain variables for measuring the entrepreneurship rate. In particular cases like entrepreneurship inside the universities and its application in processes of entrepreneurial incubation, the availability of primary information turns out to be more precarious (Kantis, Postigo, Federico & Tamborini, 2002).

4.2 Big Data: A New Generation of Data-driven Organizations

Big Data refers to the confluence of a variety of technological tools for the management of structured, semi-structured and unstructured data produced by society and organizations. These technologies have been maturing since the beginning of the first decade of the twenty-first century, but their boom has been expanding and growing since 2010, mainly with the growth of social networks and the exponential generation of unstructured data[1] in society and recently in organizations

(Aguilar, 2016; Gobble, 2013; Wamba et al., 2015; Chen, Chiang & Storey, 2012: 1167; Schiller et al., 2014).

The literature associated with the subject of Big Data and its application is relatively broad; however, the vast majority of studies that have been conducted are literary reviews, followed by research in the area of analytics and applications of statistical methods for data analysis, and finally, in a smaller proportion, empirical case studies that analyze the results of implemented technological projects (Wamba et al., 2015; Chen & Zhang, 2014). There is also an extensive bibliography that analyzes the progress of technologies related to Big Data over the past two decades, as well as the limitations that have been found for its implementation (Kim, Trimi & Chung, 2014; Cheng et al., 2012). Finally, there are studies related to decision-making processes and their relationship with information management in organizations. These studies focus on analyzing the evolution of organizational culture based on data and its impact on the increase of productivity and the profitability of institutions (McAffe & Brynjolfsson, 2012; Horita, Albuquerque, Marchezini & Merdiondo, 2017; Kościelniaka & Puto, 2015; Elgendy & Elragal, 2016).

Big Data is also known as the technology of the five "Vs", since the following five aspects are involved in the process of managing large volumes of information: (1) *Volume*, as the production of information at the global level has increased fivefold over the past five years and currently produces about 7 Zetabytes per year, much of which comes from unstructured data (Wamba et al., 2015). (2) *Variety*, due to the fact that information that organizations manage today comes from a variety of structured, semi-structured and unstructured sources, many of which are not produced inside the organization but outside it; this situation will be accentuated over time and the growth of devices connected to the Internet or IOT. (3) *Velocity*, given that organizations increasingly need real-time data to allow assertive decision making, especially given that the volume of information generated by the market grows at an exponential rate. (4) *Veracity*, since one of the most sensitive issues in data management is its reliability and validity of information, which indicate whether the results obtained from a given sample of data are replicable and generalizable for other populations and meet the falsifiability principle (Horita et al., 2017). (5) *Value*, perhaps the biggest of the five Vs, since the management of large volumes of information seeks to help organizations discard the data considered as garbage and to be able to classify, clean and process only data that adds value to decision making. In this order, value is a product of the correct analysis of the information required, the most appropriate technologies to manage it, and the identification of the purpose and scope of the data generated (Kim et al., 2014).

The question about Big Data and its contribution to decision making is whether organizations are aware of the importance of having an optimal system for managing their information. In the study by Kim et al. (2014) they found that a large number of decision makers in a sample of countries they analyzed were skeptical about the benefit of implementing Big Data tools to support their decisions. Even the authors indicate that the vast majority of initiatives regarding Big Data did not go beyond their exploratory phase.

In turn, McAffe and Brynjolfsson (2012), in their research of 330 large public sector companies in North America, found that the vast majority of top managers made their decisions intuitively or were driven by basic market data. However, the authors indicate that those organizations that showed strong decision-making orientation based on the inter-relation of different sources of information, and the correct management of their data, were on average 6 percent more productive and profitable compared to their competitors (McAffe & Brynjolfsson, 2012: 6).

This indicates that the application of Big Data tools to the decision-making process is an early stage issue that will be consolidated over the next decade. In that order, the priority for organizations regarding the management of their information is to determine their real needs in relation to the processing of data, and how they generate "value" for the different stakeholders involved. Following McAffe and Brynjolfsson (2012), it is a question of prioritizing the knowledge based on the information generated on the personal beliefs of management teams in each institution, transforming the organizational culture guided by the unfounded assumptions of the context.

The key to generating value-added from data is to establish what kind of information organizations should generate to respond to the changing needs of their key players. What will matter in the future is not the ability of an organization to generate information but its ability to interrelate different data sources (structured, semi-structured and un-structured) in order to predict the preferences of its consumers and providers (Kim et al., 2014).

Some studies (Mallinger & Stefl, 2015; Schiller et al., 2015: 812; Chen & Zhang, 2014: 318) indicate that the decision making based on Big Data tools requires a systematic process prior to the technological implementation that incorporates: (1) an analysis and exhaustive discovery of information with which it is counted and integrated; (2) cleaning and standardization of data that will be analyzed in the future in order to prevent setbacks; (3) selection and identification of the appropriate technological tools, and (4) defining the scope regarding the types of decisions generated based on the information (operational, tactical or strategic).

This case study will explain how the process was carried out using data from the GEM, leaving for the final discussion the necessity to establish to what extent the Big Data App does or does not allow for a deeper study of entrepreneurship worldwide and its correlation with the macroeconomic and systemic conditions of the participating countries.

4.3 Data

The information the GEM has been collecting for about the past 18 years is growing and it is currently difficult to manage this information using traditional techniques. The GEM requires new forms of processing its data to enable enhanced decision making. These are the characteristics of a Big Data project as a new way to reuse and extract value from information (Curry, 2016). Accordingly, the characteristics of the data used in this project are described in detail below.

4.3.1 Global Entrepreneurship Monitor

The Big Data App of the GEM includes information from the Adult Population Survey (APS) and the National Expert Survey (NES) at national and individual level for the sample. The individual level refers to raw data of individuals surveyed and the national level refers to a set of indicators established at the individual level (rates). The conceptual model and detailed descriptions of these tools may be found in Reynolds et al. (2005: 206–212).

Each year the data team of the GEM collected approximately 25,000 cases of adult population surveyed and 75 experts by country. It can be seen from the above analysis that, over 15 years, the data for about 100 countries will be 3,750,000 cases and if we multiply this data by the number of questions, we are talking about 386,250,000 variables available for analysis (see Table 4.1).

Table 4.1 Estimated Data of GEM: 100 Countries, 2000–2015

Survey: Individual Level	Cases/Year	Cases/15 Years	Number of Questions
APS	25,000	3,750,000	103
NES	75	112,500	185

Source: Own elaboration using data from www.gemconsorcium.org.

Table 4.2 Sample: Six Countries, 2000–2015

Survey		Cases	Variables
APS	Individual	2,81,726	2,084
	National	80	1,002
NES	Individual	2,045	1,862
	National	77	1,742

Source: Developed by the author based on descriptive analysis of sample.

It is important to note, however, that a sample of five countries was used in the pilot phase: Germany, South Africa, Argentina, Israel and Malaysia, equivalent to 2,81,726 cases for APS and 2,045 cases for NES. The decision to take a sample allowed us to streamline the processing of data and its integration due to the challenge of the standardization of data (Table 4.2).

4.3.2 World Bank Data

The World Bank group is one of the world's largest sources of funding and knowledge for developing countries. This group has a large trajectory collecting data concerning economic and human development. In Table 4.3 we present a sample of the most important datasets (there are more in https://datacatalog.worldbank.org/search/datasets) with the objective of estimating the volume and variety of that information.

Regarding volume, the WB has nearly 14,319 indicators as a part of its open data. Each indicator needs data for denominator and numerator (each one components of a rate) for its construction, calculated from microdata, then the needs of data related to an indicator of growth.

Regarding variety, the WB has structured information presented by datasets, databases, pre-formatted tables, reports and other sources. Table 4.3 presents a sample (15 percent) of the most used databases of the 69 databases available as open data WB. Table 4.3 summarizes information from an average of 200 countries, 7,123 data series, collected through an average of 45 years.

As an example, the World Development Indicator is the World Bank's premier compilation of cross-country comparable data on development (see Table 4.4). The database contains more than 1,400 time series indicators for 217 economies and more than 40 country groups, with data for many indicators going back more than 50 years. World Development Indicators include data spanning 56 years, from 1960–2016.

Table 4.3 A Sample of World Bank Databases by Country and Number of Years Available

World Bank Databases	Country	Series	Time
World Development Indicators	264	1,574	58
Statistical Capacity Indicators	154	29	14
Education Statistics: All Indicators	242	3,665	65
Gender Statistics	263	631	58
Health Nutrition and Population Statistics	259	374	58
Poverty and Equity	184	44	43
Doing Business	258	59	15
IDA Results Measurement System	92	51	28
Millennium Development Goals	263	132	26
Quarterly Public Sector Debt	87	564	91
Subtotal	**2,066**	**7,123**	**456**

Source: Developed with data based on WB databases (https://data.worldbank.org/indicator).

The structure of information comprises a three-stage model. For example, the topic worldview has five subtopics, and each one has a group of indicators. Table 4.5 presents a disaggregation level of worldview information, which includes 40 indicators in its five subtopics.

For the pilot phase of the Big Data GEM project, the information from World Bank Indicators was considered with the goal to improve the understanding of the relationship between entrepreneurship and the economic context to add value to national teams. More than 50 new World Bank Indicators were included in the current version of the Big Data App. This improvement is useful for multiple comparisons with GEM indicators as well as for public policy analysis.

4.3.3 Social Networking and Microblogging Service Data

The App allows for text and sentiment analysis with Google Trends, Twitter and blogs. Text analysis tools can be used to understand patterns in unstructured data. The way these tools work is by tokenizing strings of characters and applying different measures to them such as counts, co-occurrence of words, and correlation of words with the goal of determining positive, negative and neutral sentiments for a document (Pak & Paroubek, 2010; Agarwal et al., 2011).

We used a free sample of 25,000 tweets and 1,000 blogs in the English language with words related to entrepreneurship. The purpose

Table 4.4 Topics and Subtopics of WDI

Topic	Description	Subtopics
Worldview	Presents indicators that measure worldview.	5
Poverty and Shared Prosperity	Presents indicators that measure progress towards the World Bank group's twin goals of ending extreme poverty by 2030 and promoting shared prosperity in every country.	5
People	Showcases indicators covering education, health, jobs, social protection and gender, and provides a portrait of societal progress across the world.	21
Environment	Presents indicators on the use of natural resources, such as water and energy, and various measures of environmental degradation, including pollution, deforestation and loss of habitat, all of which must be considered in shaping development strategies.	14
Economy	Provides a window on the global economy through indicators that describe the economic activity of the more than 200 countries and territories that produce, trade and consume the world's output.	17
States and Markets	Encompasses indicators on private investment and performance, financial system development, quality and availability of infrastructure, and the role of the public sector in nurturing investment and growth.	16
Global links	Presents indicators on the size and direction of the flows and links that enable economies to grow, including measures of trade, remittances, equity and debt, as well as tourism and migration.	16
Total		**94**

Source: Own elaboration, using information from WDI.

of this analysis was to test the hypothesis or multiple relationships between variables of expectations and motivations of entrepreneurs for the six countries. Table 4.6 presents the possible hypothesis related to motivations and expectations of entrepreneurs.

Table 4.5 Disaggregation Level of Topic: Worldview

Size of the Economy	**Women in Development**
1 Population	1 Life expectancy at birth
2 Surface area	2 Women who were first married by age 18
3 Population density	3 Account at a financial institution
4 Gross national income, Atlas method	4 Wage and salaried workers
5 Gross national income per capita, Atlas method	5 Wage and salaried workers
6 Purchasing power parity gross national income	6 Firms with female participation in ownership
7 Gross domestic product	7 Women in parliaments

Size of the Economy
1 Population
2 Surface area
3 Population density
4 Gross national income, Atlas method
5 Gross national income per capita, Atlas method
6 Purchasing power parity gross national income
7 Gross domestic product

Global Goals: Ending Poverty and Improving Lives
1 Percentage share of income or consumption
2 Prevalence of child malnutrition
3 Maternal mortality ratio
4 Under-five mortality rate
5 Incidence of HIV
6 Incidence of tuberculosis
7 Mortality caused by road traffic injury
8 Primary completion rate
9 Contributing family workers
10 Labor productivity

Strengthening Partnership
1 Official development assistance (ODA) by donor
2 Least developed countries' access to high-income markets
3 Support to agriculture

Women in Development
1 Life expectancy at birth
2 Women who were first married by age 18
3 Account at a financial institution
4 Wage and salaried workers
5 Wage and salaried workers
6 Firms with female participation in ownership
7 Women in parliaments
8 Non-discrimination clause mentions gender in the constitution

Global Goals: Promoting Sustainability
1 People using safely managed drinking water services
2 People using safely managed sanitation services
3 Access to electricity
4 Renewable energy consumption
5 Expenditures for R&D
6 Urban population living in slums
7 Ambient PM2.5 air pollution
8 Adjusted net savings
9 Carbon dioxide emissions
10 Nationally protected terrestrial and marine areas
11 Intentional homicides
12 Internet use

Source: Own elaboration using WBI data.

Considering the complexity of the relationship between entrepreneurship and other variables at different levels, we experimented with some others, such as entrepreneurship and financing, entrepreneurship and failure, and others that we present in the results section below.

The sentiment analysis with social networking was developed from blogs about entrepreneurship, Twitter data and GEM reports (at exploratory levels), due to the time and cost constraints associated with the project.

Table 4.6 Hypothesis Related to Motivations and Expectations of Entrepreneurs

Key Motivators:	To continue with the family business
	To improve personal or family income
	Necessity: they did not find a job as employees
	Autonomy: they wanted to be independent
	Flexibility of work conditions
	Development of professional career
	Dismissal from their last job
	Identification of a business opportunity
	Previous training or expertise in the sector
Key Expectations:	To increase company sales
	To increase business profits
	To improve the quality or innovation of products or services
	To increase market participation
	To export or maintain presence in international markets
	To enhance the brand positioning and "top of mind"
	To benefit society or vulnerable groups
	To benefit the conservation of environment
	Business sustainability and growth over time
	To increase the number of created jobs
Key Aspects for Self–Efficacy:	Creativity
	Audacity
	Passion
	Leadership
	Innovation
	Future vision
	Efficacy
	Technical skills
	Soft skills
	Management skills
	Resilience
	Persuasion
	Assume calculated risks
	Environmental analysis
	Social and environmental sensitivity
	A low fear of failure
Key Perceptions of Entrepreneurs Related to Limitations/ Restrictions of the Entrepreneurial Ecosystem:	Lack of funding
	Business regulations and taxes
	Lack of government entrepreneurship programs
	Corruption
	Low integration of private and public sector
	Precarious commercial and legal infrastructure
	Entry regulation
	Cultural and social norms

Source: Own elaboration.

4.4 Methodology

The the Big Data App project was proposed in two phases: (1) A first pilot phase, which was designed to develop the prototype of the Big Data App for six countries in order to improve the visualization and processing of GEM data and its interrelation with external data sources (structured and unstructured), and (2) A second phase of scalability whose purpose would be to implement the full version of the App for the nearly 100 countries affiliated to the GEM improving the user interface and introducing new functionalities and external data sources. The current methodology corresponds to the pilot phase.

The project was developed from a data quality approach, because we believe that the quality of the Big Data App depends on the quality of data. Accordingly, we adopt the "Big Data Value Chain" methodology across all projects.

4.4.1 Design

Figure 4.1 presents the methodology used to develop the project. As Caffo, Peng and Leek (2016: 15–20) recommend in their book *Data Science Executive*, all data science projects begin with the "question" which implies the identification of the problem and needs. Once the first step is clear it is able to design a matrix of planning when the time and costs are critical to define.

The second step uses approximately 80 percent of execution. The data processing or tidying data is the most important process in the Big Data Project, because "if garbage in, garbage out". Activities such as data cleaning, database review, standardization variables and labels, data tidying, exploring and verifying the compatibility of data with GEM databases and integration are activities that few decision makers see as strategic for the success of this kind of project (see Figure 4.1).

4.4.2 Implementation

One of the main uses of Big Data platforms is the ability to easily visualize the different indicators and variables from different data sources (structured and unstructured) related to entrepreneurship. The process of the implementation of the Big Data App with GEM data begins with the definition of data structure, data integration of external sources and developing code in R and Java. R programming language is the standard in the BD ecosystem and Java is the standard in the web ecosystem.

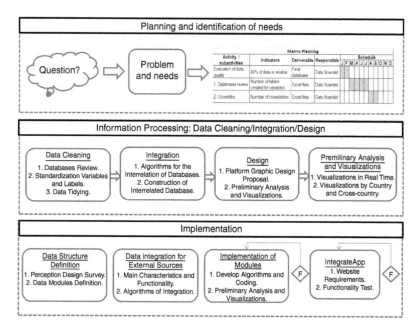

Figure 4.1 Methodology of Big Data and Entrepreneurship Project.

Source: Developed by the authors.

Table 4.7 Results of the Perception Design Survey

Main Characteristics of Platform	*Functionality*
The data visualization and versatility of the tool to compare countries and regions in different dimensions over time.	Comparative analysis by countries, regions and dimensions over time
The Big Data App must allow users to interrelate the data at individual levels with the national level using APS and NES easily.	Integrate individual and national level
The structured external data sources users perceive that could provide relevant information on entrepreneurship.	Integrate information of the World Bank, Doing Business and World Economic Forum
Users perceive that the unstructured data (such as blogs and Twitter) could provide relevant information about the sentiments, motivations and aspirations of entrepreneurs regarding their business life cycle.	Integrate information from blogs and Twitter

Source: Developed by the authors.

The data structure definition refers to the design and programming of the user interface of the Big Data App of the GEM. A perception design survey for the GERA team (experts) was developed to collect a list of requirements related to platform design. The main result of this survey is given in Table 4.7 and is related to a comparison of different variables and different sources, and visualization by country, region and time.

4.5 Discussion

A continued process of feedback was practiced during the project in order to satisfy customers' requirements. The first feedback was related to functionalities of the Big Data App. In this case we apply the survey to an expert team of the GEM, with results presented in Table 4.7. The needs of the GEM are a strong comparative analysis by countries, regions, dimensions along the timeline, integrating individual and national level data, and integrating structured external (WBI) and unstructured (Twitter and blogs) sources.

Another moment of feedback intervention from team experts was improving user interface and enhancing visualizations of GEM data. The numbers of variables and dimensions presented in the user interface are critical for the final user, in this case the GEM team members in each country. The space and types of visualizations required constant review until completion of the final version. Finally, the implementation of the Big Data application faced a lot of challenges in its pilot phase for GEM researchers as well as for the GEM as a global project. Some of these challenges are as follows:

- The first challenge in Big Data projects is their scalability and finding the added value that the applications could have for organizations in the short and medium term, and continues to be under discussion in the GEM project.
- Enhancing the user interface is always the other issue in Big Data applications due to the fact that user environments of this technology are still in the early stages, and this aspect will be resolved in coming years.
- Perhaps a great challenge for projects like this is to resolve the question: How to create value for different stakeholders and users involved with the technology? In order to answer, we have to respond first to the question: What are the particular needs of each stakeholder regarding information management?

- Finally, the big challenge is for data standardization to be integrated with multiple data sources (structured, semi-structured and unstructured). If organizations understand that standardized data is crucial to guarantee the "veracity" of the information, the next steps regarding the adoption of Big Data technologies could be made easier.

Note

1 Unstructured data (or unstructured information) is information that either does not have a pre-defined data model or is not organized in a pre-defined manner. Unstructured information is typically text-heavy but may also contain data such as dates, numbers and facts. This results in irregularities and ambiguities that make it difficult to understand using traditional programs as compared to data stored in fielded form in databases or annotated (semantically tagged) in documents.

(https://en.wikipedia.org/wiki/Unstructured_data)

References

Acs, Z. J. & Szerb, L. (2007). Entrepreneurship, economic growth and public policy. *Small Business Economics*, 28(2–3), 109–122.

Acs, Z., Astebro, T., Audretsch, D. & Robinson, T. (2016). Public policy to promote entrepreneurship: A call to arms. *Small Business Economics*, 47, 35–51. DOI. 10.1007/s11187-016-9712-2.

Agarwal, A., Xie, B., Vovsha, I., Rambow, O. & Passonneau, R. (2011). Sentiment analysis of Twitter data. In *Proceedings of the Workshop on Languages in Social Media* (pp. 30–38). Association for Computational Linguistics, UK.

Aguilar, L. J. (2016). *Big Data, Análisis de grandes volúmenes de datos en organizaciones*. Alfaomega Grupo, Madrid.

Álvarez, P., García, S. I., Menéndez, C., Federico, J. & Kantis, H. (2016). El ecosistema emprendedor de la Ciudad Autónoma de Buenos Aires. Una mirada exploratoria. *Pymes, Innovación y Desarrollo*, 4(1). UBA, Buenos Aires, Argentina.

Anghelache, C., Anghel, M. G. & Solomon, A. G. (2017). National accounts system: Source of information in macroeconomic forecast. *International Journal of Academic Research in Accounting, Finance and Management Sciences*, 7(2), 76–82.

Argote, M. & Parra, L. (2016) Marco conceptual para el análisis de brechas tecnológicas en el sector metalmecánico. In L. Parra, *Análisis de brechas tecnológicas en el sector metalmecánico desde el estudio de casos de contraste*. EAN University, Bogotá, p. 95.

Audretsch, D. (2012). Entrepreneurship research. *Management Decision*, 50(5), 755–764.

Autio, E., Rannikko, H., Handelberg, J. & Kiuru, P. (2014). *Analyses on the Finnish High-Growth Entrepreneurship Ecosystem.* Aalto University Publication Series BUSINESS + ECONOMY, 1.

Belitski, M., Chowdhury, F. & Desai, S. (2016). Taxes, corruption, and entry. *Small Business Economics,* 47(1), 201–216.

Benavente, J. M. & Crespi, G. (2016). Towards a theoretical approach to national systems of innovation. *Estudios de Economía,* 22(2), 243.

Caffo, B., Peng, R. D. & Leek, R. H. (2016). *Executive Data Science: A Guide to Training and Managing the Best Data Scientists.* Lean Publishers, Victoria, BC.

Canibano, L. & Sánchez, M. P. (2009). Intangibles in universities: Current challenges for measuring and reporting. *Journal of Human Resource Costing & Accounting,* 13(2), 93–104.

Chen, C. L. P. & Zhang, C-Y. (2014). Data-intensive applications, challenges, techniques and technologies: A survey on Big Data. *Information Sciences,* 275, 314–347.

Chen, H., Chiang, R. H. & Storey, V. C. (2012). Business intelligence and analytics: From big data to big impact. *MIS Quarterly,* 36(4), 1165–1188.

Crespi, G., Katz, J. & Olivari, J. (2017). Innovation, natural resource-based activities and growth in emerging economies: The formation and role of knowledge-intensive service firms. *Innovation and Development,* 1–23.

Curry, E. (2016). The Big Data value chain: Definitions, concepts, and theoretical approaches. In J. Cavanillas, E. Curry & W. Wahlster (eds), *New Horizons for a Data-driven Economy.* Springer, Champaign, IL.

Eatwell, J. (2016). International capital liberalization: The impact on world development. *Estudios de economia,* 24(2), 219.

Elgendy, N. & Elragal, A. (2016). Big Data analytics in support of the decision-making process. *Procedia Computer Science,* 100, 1071–1084.

Estrin, S. & Mickiewicz, T. (2013). Entrepreneurship in transition economies: The role of institutions and generational change. In M. Miniti, *The Dynamics of Entrepreneurship: Evidence from the Global Entrepreneurship Monitor Data.* Oxford University Press, Oxford, pp. 181–208.

Fuerlinger, G., Fandl, U. & Funke, T. (2015). The role of the state in the entrepreneurship ecosystem: Insights from Germany. *Triple Helix,* 2(1), 3.

Gobble, M. A. (2013) Big Data: The next big thing in innovation. *Research and Technology Management,* 56(1), 64–66.

Hausman, D., McPherson, M. & Satz, D. (2016). *Economic Analysis, Moral Philosophy, and Public Policy.* Cambridge University Press, Cambridge.

Horita, F. E., de Albuquerque, J. P., Marchezini, V. & Mendiondo, E. M. (2017). Bridging the gap between decision-making and emerging big data sources: An application of a model-based framework to disaster management in Brazil. *Decision Support Systems,* 97, 12–22.

Iamsiraroj, S. (2016). The foreign direct investment–economic growth nexus. *International Review of Economics & Finance,* 42, 116–133.

Kantis, H., Federico, J. & Ibarra, S. (2014). Índice de condiciones sistémicas para el emprendimiento dinámico. In *Una herramienta para la acción en America Latina.* BID, Washington, DC.

Kantis, H., Postigo, S., Federico, J. & Tamborini, F. (2002). El surgimiento de emprendedores de base universitaria: en qué se diferencian? Evidencias empíricas para el caso de Argentina. In *Presentado en: RENT XVI Conference, Barcelona.*

Katz, J. (2017). The Latin American transition from an inward-oriented industrialization strategy to a natural resource-based model of economic growth. *Institutions and Economies,* 7(1), 9–22.

Kelley, D., Singer, S. & Herrington, M. (2016). *2015/2016 Global Report.* GEM Global Entrepreneurship Monitor, Babson College, Universidad del Desarrollo, Universiti Tun Abdul Razak, Tecnológico de Monterrey, International Council for Small Business (ICSB).

Kim, G. H., Trimi, S. & Chung, J. H. (2014). Big-data applications in the government sector. *Communications of the ACM,* 57(3), 78–85.

Kościelniaka, H. & Puto, A. (2015). BIG DATA in decision making processes of enterprises. *Procedia Computer Science,* 65, 1052–1058.

Leyden, D. P. & Link, A. N. (2013). Knowledge spillovers, collective entrepreneurship, and economic growth: The role of universities. *Small Business Economics,* 41(4), 797–817.

Leyden, D. P. & Link, A. N. (2014). A theoretical analysis of the role of social networks in entrepreneurship. *Resources Policy,* 43(7), 1157–1163.

Link, A. N. & Link, J. R. (2007). *Government as Entrepreneur.* Oxford University Press, New York.

Mallinger, M. & Stefl, M. (2015). Big Data decision making. *Graziadio Business Review,* 18(2).

Martinez-Lopez, L. & Martinez-Lopez, F. J. (2010). Intelligent e-services and multi-agent systems for B2C e-commerce. *Internet Research,* 20(3).

McAfee, A. & Brynjolfsson, E. (2012). Big data: The management revolution. *Harvard Business Review,* 90(10), 60–68.

Minniti, M. (2013). *The Dynamics of Entrepreneurship: Evidence from Global Entrepreneurship Monitor Data.* Oxford University Press, Oxford.

Navicke, J., Rastrigina, O. & Sutherland, H. (2014). Nowcasting indicators of poverty risk in the European Union: A microsimulation approach. *Social Indicators Research,* 119(1), 101–119.

Nunns, J. & Rosenthal, S. (2016). Financial transaction taxes in theory and practice. *National Tax Journal,* 69(1), 171–216.

Obschonka, M. (2017). The quest for the entrepreneurial culture: Psychological Big Data in entrepreneurship research. *Current Opinion in Behavioral Sciences,* 18, 69–74.

Ostrom, E. (2014). Collective action and the evolution of social norms. *Journal of Natural Resources Policy Research,* 6(4), 235–252.

Pak, A. & Paroubek, P. (2010). Twitter as a corpus for sentiment analysis and opinion mining. *LREc,* 10, 1320–1326.

Parra, L. & Piñeros, A. (2016) ¿Cuál es el rol del Estado en la promoción del Sector Metalmecánico en Colombia? In L. Parra, *Análisis de brechas tecnológicas en el sector metalmecánico desde el estudio de casos de contraste* (p. 95). Ed. EAN University, Bogotá.

Reynolds, P. D., Camp, S. M., Bygrave, W. D., Autio, E. & Hay, M. (2001). *GEM Global Entrepreneurship Report, 2001 Summary Report.* Kauffman Center for Entrepreneurial Leadership at the Ewing Marion Kauffman Foundation, Kansas City, KA.

Reynolds, P. D., Bosma, N., Autio, E., Hunt, S., De Bono, N., Servais, I., Lopez-Garcia, P. & Chin, N. (2005). Global Entrepreneurship Monitor: Data collection design and implementation 1998–2003. *Small Business Economics*, 24(3), 205–231.

Rothaermel, F. T., Agung, S. D. & Jiang, L. (2007). University entrepreneurship: A taxonomy of the literature. *Industrial and Corporate Change*, 16(4), 691–791.

Schiller, S., Goul, M., Iyer, L., Sharda, R. & Schrader, D. (2014). Panel: Build Your Dream (not just Big) Analytics Program. In *Proceedings of the Twentieth Americas Conference on Information Systems (AMCIS)*, Savannah, GA.

Schiller, S., Goul, M., Iyer, L. S., Sharda, R., Schrader, D. & Asamoah, D. (2015). Build Your Dream (not just Big) Analytics Program. *Communications of the Association for Information Systems*, 37(40). Available at http://aisel.aisnet.org/cais/vol37/iss1/40.

Schroeck, R., Shockley, J., Smart, D., Romero-Morales, P. & Tufano (2012). Analytics: The real-world use of big data. How innovative enterprises extract value from uncertain data. IBM Institute for Business Value. Retrieved from www-03.ibm.com/systems/hu/resources/the_real_word_use_of_big_data.pdf.

Stiglitz, J. E. & Greenwald, B. C. (2016). *La creación de una sociedad del aprendizaje: Una nueva aproximación al crecimiento, el desarrollo y el progreso social.* La Esfera de los Libros, Madrid.

Wamba, S. F., Akter, S., Edwards, A., Chopin, G. & Gnanzou, D. (2015). How "big data" can make big impact: Findings from a systematic review and a longitudinal case study. *International Journal of Production Economics*, 165, 234–246.

Index

For Product Safety Concerns and Information please contact our EU representative GPSR@taylorandfrancis.com
Taylor & Francis Verlag GmbH, Kaufingerstraße 24, 80331 München, Germany

www.ingramcontent.com/pod-product-compliance
Ingram Content Group UK Ltd.
Pitfield, Milton Keynes, MK11 3LW, UK
UKHW021822240425
457818UK00006B/34